WORLD
WAR IV

DOUBLEDAY

New York   London   Toronto   Sydney   Auckland

WORLD WAR IV

THE LONG STRUGGLE

AGAINST ISLAMOFASCISM

NORMAN

PODHORETZ

PUBLISHED BY DOUBLEDAY

Copyright © 2007 by Norman Podhoretz

Published in the United States by Doubleday,
an imprint of The Doubleday Broadway Publishing Group,
a division of Random House, Inc., New York.
www.doubleday.com

DOUBLEDAY and the portrayal of an anchor with a dolphin
are registered trademarks of Random House, Inc.

Book design by Fritz Metsch

Library of Congress Cataloging-in-Publication Data
Podhoretz, Norman.
World War IV : the long struggle against Islamofascism /
by Norman Podhoretz.—1st ed.
p. cm.
Includes bibliographical references and index.
1. War on Terrorism, 2001– 2. United States—Foreign relations—
2001– I. Title. II. Title: World War 4. III. Title: World War Four.
HV6432.P63 2007
973.931—dc22   2007002741

ISBN 978-0-385-52221-2

PRINTED IN THE UNITED STATES OF AMERICA

3   5   7   9   10   8   6   4

To my newest and dearly beloved grandchildren,
Shayna and Shiri Podhoretz,
who, I pray, will be there to celebrate
our victory in World War IV

CONTENTS

PROLOGUE

DEAR READER:

As I write in the fall of 2006, exactly five years have passed since 9/11, and by the time you read this, another year or more will have gone by. There is no telling what will happen between now and then: how many changes will occur and what new conditions they might create. And yet it seems to me that the fifth anniversary of the war we have been fighting since September 11, 2001, is a singularly appropriate moment for a pause during which we can step back from the relentless daily onslaught of both details and their often tendentious or partisan interpretation and remind ourselves of the context in which such details can be put into perspective and related to one another.

This is what I will try to do in the pages that follow, and I will try to do it by piecing together the story of what this nation began fighting to accomplish even as the toxic dust was still settling on the gaping wound that would soon become known as Ground Zero. But telling the story properly will require more than a straight narrative leading from 9/11/2001 to 9/11/2006. For one thing, I will have to interrupt the narrative repeatedly in order to confront and clear away the many misconceptions, distortions, and outright falsifications that have been perpetrated over the past five years. In addition, I will be broadening the focus so as to make it possible to see why the great struggle into which the United States was plunged by 9/11 can only be understood if we think of it as World War IV.

As I say, much that neither I nor anyone else can foresee will have happened by the time you get to read these words. Even so, my guess is that one big thing will remain the same, and that is that many (most?) Americans will still be finding it hard to decide what the terrorist assault of 9/11 really meant. If my guess is right, the questions that refuse to stop nagging us today even after five full years of the war will still be in the American air after six and seven and eight: Why were we attacked? By whom exactly, and to what end? Could it have been prevented? Should we have responded, as we had to terrorist attacks in the past, by turning the problem over to cops, lawyers, and judges instead of sending in the Marines? Why did we have to invade Afghanistan? Was our subsequent invasion of Iraq part of or a distraction from the war on terrorism? Should we have taken on Iran and/or Syria instead? In any case, was the democratization of such despotic regimes, let alone the reform of Islam, a feasible objective within the foreseeable future, or were these foolishly naive utopian fantasies? And what about Israel? How did it fit into the whole picture?

I BELIEVE THAT it is impossible to arrive at satisfactory answers to such questions without—as the saying goes—connecting all the dots. And when the dots are connected, what emerges is the inescapable recognition that 9/11 constituted an open declaration of war on the United States and that the war into which it catapulted us was nothing less than another world war.

To me this seems indisputable, and yet everywhere I look (and I strongly suspect that this will still be true for you as well), I come upon people who vehemently repudiate any such interpretation of what 9/11 meant. Some of them maintain that fighting against terrorism hardly even rises to the level of a small war, much less a world war. "While terrorists are a real concern," says Andrew Mack, a prominent specialist in the study of conflict, "they have killed far fewer people than wars." And according to Professor Mack, even on the dubious assumption that we actually are at war, to represent it as global in scope "is absolute nonsense."

Now, it is, of course, true that terrorists have (thus far) murdered many fewer people than were killed in any of the world wars that have gone before. But it is also true that on 9/11 the terrorists of Al Qaeda succeeded in attacking us on our own soil—a feat that neither Kaiser Wilhelm nor Adolf Hitler nor Joseph Stalin ever managed to pull off. Furthermore, the chances are greater now than they were during the cold war that nuclear weapons will come into play. The reason is that in confronting suicide bombers and political leaders like Iran's president Ahmadinejad who are not restrained by the risk of annihilation, we cannot rely on the kind of deterrence (mutual assured destruction, or MAD) that kept both the Soviet and American nuclear arsenals in their silos during the cold war. As Bernard Lewis, the leading contemporary authority on the history and culture of the broader Middle East, says in speaking of Ahmadinejad:

> MAD, mutual assured destruction, [was effective] right through the cold war. Both sides had nuclear weapons. Neither side used them, because both sides knew the other would retaliate in kind. This will not work with a religious fanatic [like Ahmadinejad]. For him, mutual assured destruction is not a deterrent, it is an inducement. We know already that they do not give a damn about killing their own people in great numbers. We have seen it again and again.* In the final scenario, and this applies all the more strongly if they kill large numbers of their own people, they are

---

* In this connection Youssef Ibrahim of the *New York Sun* reminds us that between 1980 and 1988 in its war with Iraq, "Iran lost nearly one million of its citizens without blinking." In the words of one historical account, "A substantial proportion of these losses were incurred when Iran sent massive numbers of older men, children, and sometimes women as human 'waves' against Iraq's better-equipped forces. Although thousands upon thousands of these poorly armed forces were slaughtered with each assault, the Iranian government continued to send them to the front."

doing them a favor. They are giving them a quick free pass to heaven and all its delights. . . .*

Nor are they inhibited by a love of country:

We do not worship Iran, we worship Allah. For patriotism is another name for paganism. I say let this land [Iran] burn. I say let this land go up in smoke, provided Islam emerges triumphant in the rest of the world.

These were the words of the Ayatollah Khomeini, who ruled Iran from 1979 to 1989, and there is no reason to suppose that his disciple Ahmadinejad feels any differently.

What this means is that the once "unthinkable" nuclear holocaust has become more terrifyingly thinkable than it ever was in the past.

Still, no less an authority than the eminent British military historian Sir John Keegan agrees with Professor Mack's assessment. In the midst of the battle that erupted in the summer of 2006—when the terrorists of Hezbollah who had created a state within a state in southern Lebanon began (among other things) to launch missiles across the border and into Israel—Keegan was asked to consider whether, as some were then speculating, this "conflagration [was] a repeat of the escalating global hostilities of almost a century ago." Nothing of the kind, he emphatically replied: there could be no comparison between what was "happening today to the events that launched the great powers of Europe into World War I in 1914."

Having dismissed the analogy with World War I, Keegan took even more heated issue with the idea that we might instead be in the early stages of World War III. This idea had belatedly come to Newt

---

* Lewis was not being metaphorical here. According to the London-based "pan Arab" daily *Al Hayyat*, "the Iranian 'human waves' . . . wore keys to Paradise around their necks as they marched through Iraqi minefields."

Gingrich, the former speaker of the House of Representatives, who was at that moment beginning a well-publicized effort to (in his own words)

> describe the scale of terrorist attacks and plots, world conflicts, and the hostile declarations by rogue states and their pursuit of nuclear weapons as an emerging Third World War.

Confronted with Gingrich's words on a radio broadcast, Keegan grew so agitated that a simple expression of disagreement would not suffice. "No! No! No! No! No!" he exclaimed in a voice seething with indignation and rage.

Well, I would certainly stipulate that the battles between Israel and Hezbollah in 2006 had nothing whatever in common with the assassination of the Austrian Archduke Ferdinand by a Serbian nationalist in 1914. Nor, once it broke out, did World War I itself look anything like the war that erupted on 9/11. But then neither did World War II bear much, if any, resemblance to World War I with its static central battlefield, its trenches, and its poison gas. Which did not prevent Hitler's invasion of Poland in 1939 from being recognized as the start of another world war.

But let me now turn to my own disagreement with Gingrich and the many other commentators who either preceded or came after him in describing our present struggle as World War III. In my view, World War III began in 1947 and ended in 1989, having been fought and won by us under the highly imprecise name of the cold war. From this it follows that the right name for the war that, as we shall see, was already being waged against us long before 9/11/2001, but that we only recognized as such in the immediate aftermath of the attacks on the World Trade Center and the Pentagon, is World War IV.

To this interpretation yet another military historian, Andrew J. Bacevich of Boston University, reacts by declaring a plague on both our houses. In an article entitled "This Is Not World War Three—or Four," he writes:

We do not live in the 1930s. Despite their bizarre professed intentions of restoring the Caliphate, Islamic radicals bear no comparison with the Nazis who yearned for Lebensraum. The beginning of wisdom lies not in imposing on to the present a contrived historical paradigm but in acknowledging the complex, sloppy, morally ambiguous sequence of events that got us here.

Here again, as with Keegan on World War I, I of course agree that there is a difference between the Nazis of the 1930s or the Communists of the late 1940s and our enemies of today (whom Keegan describes as Islamic radicals but who, for reasons that will become clear in due course, I prefer to call Islamofascists). But it is axiomatic that no analogy is perfect, and this one (as I will also try to show in due course) is less imperfect than most. In any event, it has much more to commend it than the truly far-fetched analogy Bacevich draws between George W. Bush's invasion of Iraq and Winston Churchill's calamitous Gallipoli campaign in World War I. For as we learn from Bernard Lewis, the influence first of Nazism and then of Soviet Communism had everything to do with the emergence of Islamofascism as a political force:

In the year 1940, the government of France surrendered to the Axis and formed a collaborationist government in a place called Vichy. . . . [This] meant that Syria-Lebanon—a French-mandated territory in the heart of the Arab East—was now wide open to the Nazis. The governor and his high officials in the administration in Syria-Lebanon took their orders from Vichy, which in turn took orders from Berlin. The Nazis moved in, made a tremendous propaganda effort, and were even able to move from Syria eastwards into Iraq and for a while set up a pro-Nazi, fascist regime. It was in this period that political parties were formed that were the nucleus of what later became the Baath Party. The Western Allies eventually drove the Nazis out of the Middle East and suppressed these organizations. But the war ended in 1945, and the Allies left. A few years later the Soviets moved in, established an immensely powerful presence in Egypt, Syria, Iraq and various other countries, and introduced Soviet-style political practice. The adaptation from the Nazi model to the communist model was very simple and easy, requiring only a few minor adjustments, and it proceeded pretty well. That is the origin of the Baath Party and of the kind of governments that we have been confronting in the Middle East in recent years.

Along with most libertarians and a goodly number of liberals and leftists, Bacevich detects a whole range of sinister motives lurking behind the idea that 9/11 was the start of a new world war (whether it be numbered III or IV). Thus, he lists the "attractive benefits" that accrue from the world-war paradigm to neoconservatives like me. To begin with, it "provides a reassuring sense of continuity: we've been here before, we know what we need to do, we know how it's going to end." In addition, it benefits Israel ("Israel's war is our war is freedom's war"), and this, as all the world has been led to believe, is the main reason we neoconservatives conspired to hoodwink George W. Bush, Richard Cheney, and Donald Rumsfeld into thinking that 9/11 was the first salvo in a new world war and to adopt the putatively disastrous policies that flowed from this interpretation. But according to Bacevich, the same interpretation also "has utility on the domestic front":

> It facilitates efforts to mobilize popular support for military actions undertaken in pursuit of final victory. It ratifies the claims of federal authorities who insist upon exercising "wartime" prerogatives, expanding the police powers of the state and circumscribing constitutional guarantees of due process. . . . It disciplines.

The columnist (and Reagan administration alumnus) James Pinkerton adds two more items to this parade of horrors:

> If this is a real world war, expect the era of big government to come back, and to come back with a vengeance. Federal spending

went up seven-fold during World War One, and went up seven-fold again during World War Two. . . . Needless to say, taxes went way up too. . . . Oh, and back then, there was a little thing called the draft. . . . It's hard to imagine that we could fight Gingrich's WWIII with our current small military establishment.

There is, then, no shortage of commentators who deny that 9/11 plunged us into a new world war. But it is worth noting that instead of seriously addressing the merits of the argument we neo-conservatives, along with many others, have advanced, both Bacevich and Pinkerton—and by no means they alone—accuse us of bad faith. For example, Bacevich insultingly charges that the case we make is nothing more than a convenient justification for abrogating the Bill of Rights. In similar fashion, Pinkerton, relying on historical precedent, warns that in defining the struggle as a world war, we are providing an excuse to increase federal spending, raise taxes, and bring back the draft. Yet he never bothers to mention that we strongly oppose all three of these possibilities and would fight against them tooth and nail.

Be that as it may, even if the case for believing that 9/11 plunged us into a new world war is accepted, we are still left with the problem of what this new world war should be called.

In the five years since 9/11, George W. Bush has been accused of making innumerable mistakes, most of which—as I will attempt to demonstrate later on—either were not mistakes at all or were things he never even did. But the one mistake with which he can justly be charged was his refusal from the outset to give both the enemy forces and the struggle against them their true and proper names.

At first, and for a long time afterward, Bush's preferred designation was the "Global War on Terror." But GWOT—as it mockingly, and deservedly so, became known—made no more sense than calling the enemy in World War II "the blitzkrieg" rather than "Germany," or "the dive bomber" rather than "Japan."

It seems clear that this ungainly euphemism was adopted out of two related fears. The first was that identifying the enemy as

Islamofascism, or Islamic fascism, or radical Islam, or Islamism, or some other such variant, might convey the false impression that we were taking on the entire Muslim world. And it was this same fear that explained why the president kept going out of his way to praise Islam as a great religion that had been "hijacked" by evil extremists who were violating its supposedly true nature as a "religion of peace."

Only recently—that is, nearly five years into the war—did Bush finally overcome this fear and begin using the term "Islamic fascism." But the predictable outcries from Muslim organizations and their apologists frightened him off again, and he quickly dropped the "Islamic" from his increasingly scanty references to fascism. However, not for even so brief a spell did he get over the slightly different fear that prevented him from coming right out and declaring that the struggle against this nebulous enemy should be given the name of World War IV. Yet that this was what he privately believed became obvious from the series of speeches he delivered in the weeks and months after 9/11. As we go along, I will be delving into those speeches and examining them in detail, but at this point I want only to cite one brief passage to back up my claim that the president clearly saw 9/11 as the opening salvo of World War IV. It came in the very first of the series—his address to a joint session of Congress on September 20, 2001. Referring there to the "global terrorist network" that had attacked us only ten days earlier, he said:

> We have seen their kind before. They're the heirs of all the murderous ideologies of the twentieth century. By sacrificing human life to serve their radical visions, by abandoning every value except the will to power, they follow in the path of fascism, Nazism, and totalitarianism. And they will follow that path all the way to where it ends in history's unmarked grave of discarded lies.

With these words, Bush unmistakably and unambiguously placed the war against the "global terrorist network" in the direct succession to World War II and World War III. Nevertheless he

still shied away—as he would continue to do—from simply calling it World War IV. And here is where the second fear—the fear
of confusion—came in. Since the cold war had never been widely
recognized as World War III, to speak now of World War IV
would inevitably lead to the question, "What happened to World
War III? Did I miss it?" This was precisely why Newt Gingrich,
having finally decided almost five years after 9/11 that we were indeed in a world war, would number it as the third. As James
Pinkerton correctly perceived:

> Gingrich, a smart man with a politician's gift for making compli-
> cated things simple, has chosen to go with "World War Three"
> [rather than "World War Four"]. After all, in the minds of most
> Americans, the last world war was the one that ended in 1945. So
> if there's a new world war today, it's the third one.

Perhaps Bush, being endowed with the same politician's gift,
could also have gone with World War III. Yet I strongly suspect
that what prevented him from doing so was his awareness that this
new world war would have so little in common with World War
II in the way it would have to be fought that to associate them numerically would create even more confusion than going with
World War IV.

I also strongly suspect that in this the president was influenced
by one of our leading contemporary students of military strategy,
Eliot A. Cohen of the School of Advanced International Studies at
Johns Hopkins. Writing only a few days after 9/11, Cohen suc-
cinctly elucidated the difference between World War II and the
cold war, or World War III, as he was the first recent commentator to call it*:

---

* I say "recent" because he was preceded by Alexander Solzhenitsyn in 1978, who
was in turn preceded by James Burnham. Even earlier, in a Gallup poll taken in
July 1950, 57 percent of the American people answered yes to the question "Do
you think the United States is now actually in World War III?" But for one reason or another, the idea never took hold.

The cold war was World War III, which reminds us that not all global conflicts entail the movement of multi-million-man armies, or conventional front lines on a map.

Hence, to give the name of World War III to this new war would be doubly misleading. On the one hand, it would conjure up images of battle—and, Cohen would later add, of a traditional war between nation-states—to which the new war would present no clear parallels. And it would conversely obscure the "key features," in both nature and duration, that Cohen said the new war (which he now christened World War IV) would share with the cold war (which he now renamed World War III). To wit:

> that it [will] in fact [be] global; that it will involve a mixture of violent and nonviolent efforts; that it will require mobilization of skill, expertise and resources, if not of vast numbers of soldiers; that it may go on for a long time; and that it has ideological roots.

Still, if Cohen's analysis rightly led the president to reject the name of World War III, it also led him in the wrong rhetorical direction. Unable to go with World War III because he feared misleading the American people, and deterred from going with World War IV because he feared confusing them, Bush was forced onto the path of euphemism and indirection. It was the very same path onto which he was driven by the related fear that he might seem to be declaring war on all Muslims everywhere.

Understandable though this decision may have been, the loss of clarity and focus it entailed would cost Bush dearly in the political wars at home that were destined to go hand in hand with the military campaigns abroad. The price would prove especially heavy in the acrimonious debates to come over Iraq. For the president's failure to call the enemy and the struggle by their true names would allow his political opponents to rip the battle for Iraq out of its proper context as only one front or theater in a much broader conflict and then to portray it instead as a self-contained war with no connection to 9/11 or anything else. Looking back later at the first five years of this broader conflict, its dimensions would be described by the exiled Iranian commentator Amir Taheri as constituting "a global war from Indonesia to Algeria, passing through Afghanistan, Pakistan, Saudi Arabia, Lebanon and the Palestinian territories." Also looking back at the first five years, George Weigel of the Ethics and Public Policy Center would put the same point into even more specific terms:

> The war is now being fought on multiple fronts, some of which are interconnected: there is an Afghan front, an Iraqi front, an Iranian front, a Lebanese/Syrian front, a Gaza front, a Somali front, a Sudanese front, a southeast Asian front, an intelligence front, a financial-flows front, an economic front, an energy front, and a homeland-security front. These are all fields of fire—some kinetic, others of a different sort—in the same global war, and they ought to be understood as such.

In shying away from the designation World War IV, however, the president was not alone. Indeed, even Eliot Cohen soon began distancing himself from the name he had been the first to bestow on the new world war, and he was subsequently joined by many others (including, most prominently, the former CIA director R. James Woolsey) who had originally embraced it with great enthusiasm. For a while, some of them (again including Woolsey) tried "the Long War" on for size, but it no more succeeded in taking hold than "World War IV" had managed to do. And so it came about that the great struggle into which 9/11 plunged the United States was left without a name.

In telling the story of the first five years of this great struggle in the pages that follow, I hope to show that it cannot be understood, or perhaps (God help us) even won, unless we face up to the hard truth that it is indeed World War IV; that we (and you) are still only in its early stages; and that, like World War III (which took a full forty-two years to win), it will in all probability go on for a very long time.

In World War III—as in World War II—the early stages were marked by more and greater setbacks, and fewer victories, than we suffered in the first five years of World War IV. Yet in spite of the impatience, the discouragement, and the opposition that were bred by events like the defeat of General Douglas MacArthur's troops in the Philippines in World War II or the stalemate in Korea in World War III, we as a people persisted in both of these wars for as long as it took to win them, and this is precisely what we have been called upon to do today in World War IV.

For today, in the monster with two heads, one religious and the other secular, that is accordingly best described as Islamofascism, and in the states breeding, sheltering, and financing its terrorist armory, we are once again up against a truly malignant totalitarian enemy. In World War II, the totalitarian challenge to the liberal democratic world of which we were a leading part came from the Right; in World War III, it came from the Left. Now in World War IV, it comes from a religious force that was born in the seventh century, that was schooled politically at the feet of the totalitarian ideologies of the twentieth, that went on to equip itself with the technologies of the twenty-first, and that is now striving mightily to arm itself with the weaponry of the twenty-first as well.

Furthermore, contrary to complacent assessments like the ones cited earlier of the power commanded by the Islamofascists, it can plausibly be argued that they are even more dangerous and difficult to beat than their totalitarian predecessors of World War II and World War III. "After defeating fascists and communists, can the West now defeat the Islamists?" asks Daniel Pipes of the Middle East Forum. "On the face of it," he acknowledges, our

> military preponderance makes victory seem inevitable. . . . Islamists have nothing like the military machine the Axis deployed in World War II, nor the Soviet Union during the cold war. What do the Islamists have to compare with the Wehrmacht or the Red Army? The SS or Spetznaz? The Gestapo or the KGB? Or, for that matter, to Auschwitz or the gulag?

Nevertheless, Pipes goes on, "Islamists deploy formidable capabilities . . . that go far beyond small-scale terrorism." Such as:

- A potential access to weapons of mass destruction that could devastate Western life
- A religious appeal that provides deeper resonance and greater staying power than the artificial ideologies of fascism or communism
- An impressively conceptualized, funded, and organized institutional machinery that successfully builds credibility, goodwill, and electoral success
- An ideology capable of appealing to Muslims of every size and shape, from Lumpenproletariat to privileged, from illiterates to PhDs, from the well-adjusted to psychopaths, from Yemenis to Canadians . . .
- A huge number of committed cadres. If Islamists constitute 10 percent to 15 percent of the Muslim population worldwide, they number some 125 to 200 million persons, or a far greater total than all the fascists and communists, combined, who ever lived.

But the objective of the Islamofascists is not merely to deploy these resources in order to murder as many of us as possible. Like the Nazis and the Communists before them, they are dedicated to the destruction of the freedoms we cherish and for which America stands. It is these, then, that (to paraphrase George W. Bush and a long string of his predecessors, Republican and Democratic alike) we in our turn, no less than the "greatest generation" of the 1940s and its spiritual progeny of the 1950s and after, have a responsibility to uphold and are privileged to defend.

Can we discharge that responsibility? Will we?

The answer, I believe, will depend at least as much on the war being waged on what in World War II was called the "home front" as on the bloody battles being fought by our armed forces in the Middle East. Unlike World War II, which just about everyone in America wholeheartedly supported, but like World War III, when the domestic political scene seethed with angry conflicts (especially during Vietnam and its aftermath), World War IV has given rise to a war of ideas on the home front. It is a war in which those of us who see Islamofascism as the latest mutation of the totalitarian threat to our civilization and who insist on the correlative necessity of meeting and defeating it, are pitted against those who think that the threat has been wildly exaggerated and does not in any case require a military response. In its own way, this war of ideas is no less bloody than the one being fought by our troops in the Middle East. Having broken out even while the World Trade Center was still smoldering, it got a boost with the invasion of Afghanistan in 2001, gathered steam with the invasion of Iraq in 2003, escalated with the presidential election campaign of 2004, and heated up even further with the congressional election campaign of 2006. I would be very surprised if the same war were not still raging as you read.

The question of whether and to what extent the American people of this generation can or will discharge the responsibility that 9/11 imposed on us will ultimately be answered by the outcome of this great war of ideas at home—a war so ferocious that some of us have not hesitated to describe it as nothing less than a kind of civil war. It is for that reason that it must and will play so large a role in the story I am about to tell.

CHAPTER ONE

THE 9/11 BLAME GAME

HE ATTACK CAME, both literally and metaphorically, out of the blue. Literally, in that the hijacked planes that crashed into the twin towers of the World Trade Center on the morning of September 11, 2001, had been flying in a cloudless sky so blue that it seemed unreal. I happened to be on jury duty that day, in a courthouse only a half-mile or so from what would soon be known as Ground Zero. Some time after the two planes reached their targets, we all poured into the street—just as the second tower collapsed. And this sight, as if it were not impossible to believe in itself, was made all the more incredible by the perfection of the sky stretching so beautifully over it. I felt as though I had been deposited into a scene in one of those disaster movies being filmed (as they used to say) in glorious color.

But the attack came out of the blue in a metaphorical sense as well. About a year later, in November 2002, a bipartisan "9/11 Commission" would be set up to investigate how and why such a huge event could have taken us by surprise and whether it might have been prevented. Because the commission's public hearings were not held until we were all caught up in the exceptionally poisonous presidential election campaign of 2004, they quickly degenerated into an attempt by the Democrats on the panel to demonstrate that the administration of George W. Bush had been given adequate warnings but had failed to act on them.

Reinforcing this attempt was the testimony of Richard A. Clarke, who had been in charge of the counterterrorist operation in the National Security Council under Bill Clinton and then under Bush before resigning in the aftermath of 9/11. What Clarke for all practical purposes did—both at the hearings and in his hot-off-the-press, bestselling book *Against All Enemies*—was blame Bush, who had been in office for eight months when the attack occurred, while exonerating Clinton, who had spent eight *years* doing little of any significance in response to the series of terrorist assaults on American targets in various parts of the world that were launched on his watch.

Yet according to John Lehman, one of the Republican commissioners, Clarke's original testimony, given in a closed session, had included a "searing indictment of some Clinton officials and Clinton policies." The Republican members of the commission (but not their Democratic colleagues, who seemed to have known what was coming) were therefore taken aback when, in the public hearings, Clarke omitted his earlier criticisms of Clinton and delivered a one-sided assault on Bush. Then, in a different, though related, context, the commission's final report would quote material written by Clarke while he was still in office that was inconsistent with his more recent public and much-publicized denial of any relationship whatsoever between Iraq and the Al Qaeda terrorists who had attacked us.

In a less polarized political and cultural climate, these two revelations would have discredited Clarke altogether. But so useful was he to the violently anti-Bush animus then gathering steam that he became the first in a long string of such former members of or outside consultants to the Bush administration who, no matter how seriously their credibility had been damaged, would be rewarded with fame and/or fortune for turning on the president they had once served. (I will have more to say in due course about the most notorious of these, Ambassador Joseph C. Wilson IV.)

But the point I wish to stress is not that Clarke was exaggerating or lying. It is that the attack on 9/11 did indeed come out of the blue in the sense that no one ever took such a possibility seriously enough to figure out what to do about it. Even Clarke himself, who at a meeting on July 5, 2001, warned that "something really spectacular is going to happen here, and it's going to happen soon," had to admit under questioning by one of the 9/11 commissioners that if all his recommendations had been acted upon, the attack still could not have been prevented. And in its final report, the commission, while digging up no fewer than ten episodes that with hindsight could be seen as missed "operational opportunities," thought that these opportunities could not have been acted on effectively enough to frustrate the attack. Indeed not: not, that is, in the real America as it existed at the time.

It was, to begin with, an America in which the FBI had been so hobbled by congressional restraints that it could scarcely make a move, and so intimidated by legal restrictions that it shied away from taking action even when it had very good reasons to pounce. The most egregious case in point was what happened when, only a month before 9/11, an agent in the FBI's Minneapolis field office discovered that one Zacarias Moussaui, a French citizen of Moroccan descent, had enrolled in a flight school in order to learn how to take off and land a Boeing 747. The agent initiated an investigation, which, the 9/11 Commission report would tell us, led him to conclude that Moussaui was "an Islamic extremist preparing for some future act in furtherance of radical fundamentalist goals." The agent also suspected that Moussaui was planning to hijack a plane, and to check out this suspicion he wanted to seize and search Moussaui's laptop computer. For this he needed a warrant, but his superiors at FBI headquarters in Washington did not believe that there was sufficient probable cause of a crime to obtain one. In the hope of getting around this problem, the agent and his colleagues now tried to show that Moussaui was an agent of a foreign power. This set them off on a wild-goose chase involving intelligence agencies in England and France, not to mention the CIA, the FAA, the Customs Service, the State Department, the

INS, and the Secret Service. But still no warrant. Why? Because, the 9/11 Commission report explains:

> There was substantial disagreement between Minneapolis agents and FBI headquarters [in Washington] as to what Moussaui was planning to do. In one conversation between a Minneapolis supervisor and a headquarters agent, the latter complained that Minneapolis's . . . request was couched in a manner intended to get people "spun up." The supervisor replied that was precisely his intent. He said he was "trying to keep someone from taking a plane and crashing it into the World Trade Center." The headquarters agent replied that this was not going to happen and that they did not know if Moussaui was a terrorist.

Well, the headquarters agent would eventually find out not only that Moussaui was a terrorist but that he was a member of Al Qaeda and slated to participate in a West Coast follow-up to 9/11.

As if such obstacles were not enough to block an effective counter to the threat of terrorism in pre-9/11 America, there was also the "wall of separation." This wall was erected during the Clinton administration to obstruct communication or cooperation between the FBI and the CIA. The main purpose was supposedly to prevent secret information and intelligence sources from being compromised by law enforcement agencies and prosecutors. But the idea must also have owed more than a little something to the hope among leftists and liberals that keeping the FBI and the CIA apart would reduce the menace they both allegedly posed to "dissent" and civil liberties.

Be that as it may, let me cite only three mind-boggling examples of what the "wall of separation" wrought. They come from Lawrence Wright of *The New Yorker* by way of the conveniently succinct summaries by Dexter Filkins of the *New York Times* (two publications that one would expect to be justifying the "wall of separation" and not exposing the horrendous damage it did). Here is the first:

The CIA . . . knew that high-level Qaeda operatives had held a meeting in Malaysia in January 2000, and, later, that two of them had entered the United States. Both men turned out to be part of the team that hijacked the planes on Sept. 11. The CIA failed to inform . . . the FBI—which might have been able to locate the men and break up the plot—until late in the summer of 2001.

The second such example of the damage done by the "wall of separation" is even worse:

At meetings, CIA analysts dangled photos of two of the eventual hijackers in front of FBI agents, but wouldn't tell them who they were. The FBI agents could sense that the CIA possessed crucial pieces of evidence about Islamic radicals they were investigating, but couldn't tell what they were. The tension came to a head at a meeting in New York on June 11, exactly three months before the catastrophe, which ended with FBI and CIA agents shouting at each other across the room.

And the third of the three examples may be the worst of them all:

Ali Soufan, an FBI agent assigned to Al Qaeda, was taken aside on September 12 and finally shown the names and photos of the men the CIA had known for more than a year and a half were in America. The planes had already struck. Soufan ran to the bathroom and retched.

Finally, the America of those far-off days before 9/11 was a country in which politicians and the general public alike were still unable and/or unwilling to believe that terrorism might actually represent a genuine threat. Attention was of course paid by the professionals within the federal government and in various law enforcement agencies whose job it was to keep their eyes open for possible terrorist attacks on American soil. Yet not even they could imagine that anything as big as 9/11 might be in the offing, and when the few lonely exceptions were not being stymied by the "wall of separation," the initiatives they tried to take were invariably killed off by bureaucratic bungling and inertia.

But returning to the politicians and the public, the general attitude is well captured by Lawrence Wright in the story he tells of another FBI agent named Dan Coleman. By 1998 Coleman had concluded after an extensive investigation (conducted on his own hook) that Al Qaeda "was a worldwide terror organization dedicated to destroying America, but [he] couldn't even get his superiors to return his phone calls on the matter." As if this was not disheartening enough, what most frightened Coleman about this new type of threat was that no one in America would be able to take it seriously:

> It was too bizarre, too primitive and exotic. Up against the confidence that Americans placed in modernity and technology and their own ideals to protect them from the savage pageant of history, the defiant gestures of bin Laden and his followers seemed absurd and even pathetic.

Insofar as the politicians and the general public bothered thinking about terrorism at all, they tended, like the FBI in Wright's account, to regard it "as a nuisance, not a real threat." Amazingly, this was precisely how John Kerry—running for president on the Democratic ticket more than two years after bin Laden had vindicated Coleman's apprehensions in the most spectacular terms—would nostalgically describe the pre-9/11 attitude in the course of advocating a return to it:

> We have to get back to the place we were, where terrorists are not the focus of our lives, but they're a nuisance. As a former law enforcement person, I know we're never going to end prostitution. We're never going to end illegal gambling. But we're going to reduce it, organized crime, to a level where it isn't on the rise. It isn't threatening people's lives every day, and fundamentally, it's something that you continue to fight, but it's not threatening the fabric of your life.

It was because these three conditions—legal restrictions, the wall of separation, and public indifference—prevailed in America before 9/11 that the commission was right to conclude that nothing could have been done to prevent the Al Qaeda attack. But slightly contradicting itself, the commission also said that "the 9/11 attacks were a shock, but they should not have come as a surprise." Maybe so. And yet, again, there was no one, either in government or out (and probably not even that anonymous FBI agent in Minneapolis), to whom the attacks did not come as a surprise, either in general or in the particular form they took. The commission also spoke of a "failure of imagination." Maybe so again, and yet the phrase seems inappropriate, implying as it does that success was possible. Surely a failure so widespread deserves to be considered inevitable.

To the *New York Times*, however, the failure was not at all inevitable. In a front-page editorial disguised as its own news report on the commission's final report, the *Times* credited the commission with finding that "an attack described as unimaginable had in fact been imagined, repeatedly." But not a shred of the documentary evidence cited by the *Times* for this categorical statement actually predicted that Al Qaeda would hijack commercial airliners and crash them into buildings in New York and Washington. Moreover, all of the evidence, such as it was, came from the 1990s. Nevertheless, the *Times* "report" contrived to convey the impression that in the fall of 2000 the Bush administration—then not yet even in office—had received fair warning of an imminent attack. To bolster this impression, the *Times* went on to quote from a briefing given to Bush a month before 9/11. This was only the first of a number of other ostensibly damning documents that would come to light at politically convenient moments in order to discredit Bush (while serving not so incidentally to distract attention from the larger issue at stake). Entitled "Bin Laden Determined to Strike in U.S.," the briefing in question was vague about details, confessed itself unable to "corroborate some of the more sensational threat reporting . . . that Bin Laden wanted to hijack a U.S. aircraft," and was in any case only one of many intelligence briefings with no special claim to greater authority than other, conflicting, assessments.

Interestingly, as the report of the 9/11 Commission itself noted, similar suspicions had been aroused by the surprise Japanese attack on Pearl Harbor on December 7, 1941. Since it could be shown that the then president, Franklin D. Roosevelt, had been warned by intelligence reports that the Japanese were considering just such an attack on Pearl Harbor, surely he must have known that it was coming and had chosen to do nothing about it so that he could use it as a pretext for entering into World War II. But as Roberta Wohlstetter would conclusively demonstrate in her classic book *Pearl Harbor: Warning and Decision*, Roosevelt had also been assured by other intelligence reports that it was the Panama Canal and/or the Philippines that the Japanese had in their sights. How then was he to tell, amid the "noise" of so many conflicting assessments, which, if any, to heed?

So, too, with the Bush administration. Fresh from being excoriated in separate hearings held by the Senate Intelligence Committee for invading Iraq on the basis of faulty intelligence, it was now excoriated by some of the 9/11 commissioners for not having acted on the basis of even sketchier intelligence to head off 9/11 itself. This contradiction elicited a mordant comment from Charles Hill, a former government official who had been a regular "consumer" of intelligence:

> Intelligence collection and analysis is a very imperfect business. Refusal to face this reality has produced the almost laughable contradiction of the Senate Intelligence Committee criticizing the Bush administration for acting on third-rate intelligence, even as the 9/11 Commission criticizes it for not acting on third-rate intelligence.*

---

* Hill was referring here to the hearings of the 9/11 Commission, not its final report, which did not single out the Bush administration for criticism on this score.

However, the point I most wish to stress is that there was something unwholesome, not to say unholy, about the recriminations on this issue that befouled the 9/11 Commission's public hearings and some of the interim reports by its staff. Because the recriminations had dominated the headlines for months, it came—shall we say?—both as a shock and as a surprise that this same unholy spirit was almost entirely exorcised from the commission's final report. In the end the commission agreed that no American president and no American policy could be held responsible in any degree for the aggression against the United States committed on 9/11.

Amen to that. For the plain truth is that the sole and entire responsibility rested with Al Qaeda, along with the regimes that provided it with protection and support. Furthermore, to the extent that American passivity and inaction opened the door to 9/11, neither Democrats nor Republicans, and neither liberals nor conservatives, were in a position to derive any partisan or ideological advantage. The reason, quite simply, was that much the same methods for dealing with terrorism were employed by the administrations of both parties, stretching as far back as Richard Nixon in 1970 and proceeding through Gerald Ford, Jimmy Carter, Ronald Reagan (yes, Ronald Reagan), George H. W. Bush, Bill Clinton, and right up to the pre-9/11 George W. Bush. To examine this history is to realize that even while World War III was still going on, World War IV had already begun, and that 9/11, far from being the first salvo fired at us by an enemy as implacable as any we had ever faced, actually represented the culmination of a long series of attacks that we had insisted on treating not as deliberate acts of war demanding a military response but as common crimes or the work of rogue groups operating on their own that could best be handled by the cops and the courts.

CHAPTER TWO

HOW WE EMBOLDENED
THE TERRORISTS

T HE RECORD SPEAKS dismally for itself. From 1970 to 1975, during the administrations of Nixon and Ford, several American diplomats were murdered in Sudan and Lebanon while others were kidnapped. The perpetrators were all agents of one or another faction of the Palestine Liberation Organization (PLO). A State Department report, declassified in May 2006, unwittingly conveys a good sense of how the United States reacted, or rather failed to react, to one of these incidents:

> In the early evening hours of 1 March 1973, eight Black September Organization (BSO) terrorists seized the Saudi Arabian Embassy in Khartoum as a diplomatic reception honoring the departing United States Deputy Chief of Mission (DCM) was ending. After slightly wounding the United States Ambassador and the Belgian Chargé d'Affaires, the terrorists took these officials plus the United States DCM, the Saudi Arabian Ambassador and the Jordanian Chargé d'Affaires hostage. In return for the freedom of the hostages, the captors demanded the release of various individuals, mostly Palestinian guerrillas, imprisoned in Jordan, Israel and the United States. The Khartoum operation was planned and carried out with the full knowledge and personal approval of Yasir Arafat, Chairman of the Palestine Liberation Organization (PLO), and the head of Fatah. . . . The

terrorists extended their deadlines three times, but when they became convinced that their demands would not be met and after
they reportedly had received orders from Fatah headquarters in
Beirut, they killed the two United States officials and the Belgian
Chargé.

The report concluded that

the emergence of the United States as a primary fedayeen target
indicates a serious threat of further incidents similar to that
which occurred in Khartoum.

Indeed it did, and yet the report proposed no reprisals of any kind
to the kidnapping and murder of two American diplomats, and
none was taken.*

In Israel, too, many American citizens were killed by the
PLO, though—except for the rockets fired at our embassy and
other American facilities in Beirut by the Popular Front for the
Liberation of Palestine (PFLP)—these attacks were not directly
aimed at the United States. In any case, again there were no
reprisals.

Our diplomats, then, were for some years already being murdered with impunity by Muslim terrorists when, in 1979, with
Jimmy Carter now in the White House, Iranian students—with
either the advance or subsequent blessing of the country's clerical
ruler, Ayatollah Khomeini—broke into the American embassy in
Tehran and seized fifty-two Americans as hostages. For a full five
months, Carter dithered. At last, steeling himself, he authorized a
military rescue operation that had to be aborted after a series of

---

* Only a year later, Arafat, at the invitation of the UN, would arrive in New York
accompanied by four of the terrorists who had carried out the Khartoum operation. Then, with a gun visibly strapped to his waist, he would address the
General Assembly, where his speech would be greeted with a great ovation. The
United States would oppose the invitation but would be unable (or unwilling?)
to prevent it from being extended.

mishaps that would have fit well into a Marx Brothers movie like *Duck Soup* if they had not been more humiliating than comic. After 444 days, and just hours after Reagan's inauguration in January 1981, the hostages were finally released by the Iranians, evidently because they feared that the hawkish new president might actually launch a military strike against them.

Yet if they could have foreseen what was coming under Reagan, they would not have been so fearful. In April 1983, Hezbollah—an Islamic terrorist organization that had only very recently been created by Iran and Syria and had not yet risen to the prominence it would achieve in its war against Israel in the summer of 2006—sent a suicide bomber to explode his truck in front of the American embassy in Beirut, Lebanon. Sixty-three employees, among them the Middle East CIA director, were killed and another 120 wounded. But Reagan sat still.

Six months later, in October 1983, another Hezbollah suicide bomber blew up an American barracks in the Beirut airport, killing 241 U.S. Marines in their sleep and wounding another 81. It was the bloodiest day in the history of the Marines since the battle of Iwo Jima in World War II. This time Reagan signed off on plans for a retaliatory blow, but he then allowed his secretary of defense, Caspar Weinberger, to cancel it (because it might damage our relations with the Arab world, of which Weinberger was always tenderly solicitous). Shortly thereafter, the president pulled the Marines out of Lebanon, where he had originally sent them to serve as part of a multinational peacekeeping force.

Having cut and run in Lebanon in October, Reagan again remained passive in December when the American embassy in Kuwait was bombed. Nor did he hit back when, hard upon the withdrawal of the Marines from Beirut, the CIA station chief there, William Buckley, was kidnapped by Hezbollah and then murdered. Buckley was the fourth American to be kidnapped in Beirut, and many more suffered the same fate between 1982 and 1992 (though not all died or were killed in captivity).

These kidnappings were apparently what led Reagan, who had

sworn that he would never negotiate with terrorists, to make an unacknowledged deal with Iran involving the trading of arms for hostages. But whereas the Iranians were paid off handsomely in the coin of nearly 1,500 antitank missiles (some of them sent at our request through Israel), all we got in exchange were three American hostages—not to mention the disruptive and damaging Iran-contra scandal.

In September 1984, six months after the murder of Buckley, the U.S. embassy annex near Beirut was hit by yet another truck bomb (also traced to Hezbollah). Again Reagan sat still. Or rather, after giving the green light to covert proxy retaliations by Lebanese intelligence agents, he put a stop to them when one such operation, directed against the cleric thought to be the head of Hezbollah, failed to get its main target while unintentionally killing eighty other people.

It took only another two months for Hezbollah to strike once more. In December 1984, a Kuwaiti airliner was hijacked and two American passengers employed by the U.S. Agency for International Development were murdered. The Iranians, who had stormed the plane after it landed in Tehran, promised to try the hijackers themselves but instead allowed them to leave the country. At this point, all the Reagan administration could come up with was the offer of a $250,000 reward for information that might lead to the arrest of the hijackers. There were no takers.

The following June, Hezbollah operatives hijacked still another airliner, an American one (TWA flight 847), and then forced it to fly to Beirut, where it was held for more than two weeks. During those weeks, an American naval officer aboard the plane was shot, and his body was ignominiously hurled onto the tarmac. For this the hijackers were rewarded with the freeing of hundreds of ter- rorists held by Israel in exchange for the release of the other pas- sengers. Both the United States and Israel denied that they were violating their own policy of never bargaining with terrorists, but as with the arms-for-hostages deal, and with equally good reason, no one believed them, and it was almost universally assumed that

Israel had acted under pressure from Washington. Later, four of the hijackers were caught, but only one wound up being tried and jailed (by Germany, not the United States).

The sickening beat went on. In October 1985, the *Achille Lauro*, an Italian cruise ship, was hijacked by a group under the leadership of the PLO's Abu Abbas, working with the support of Libya. One of the hijackers threw an elderly, wheelchair-bound American passenger, Leon Klinghoffer, overboard. When the hijackers attempted to escape in a plane, the United States sent Navy fighters to intercept it and force it down. Klinghoffer's murderer was eventually apprehended and sent to prison in Italy, but the Italian authorities let Abu Abbas himself go. Washington— evidently having exhausted its repertoire of military reprisals— now confined itself to protesting the release of Abu Abbas. To no avail.

Libya's involvement in the *Achille Lauro* hijacking was, however, the last free pass that country's dictator, Muammar Qaddafi, was destined to get from the United States under Reagan. In December 1985, five Americans were among the twenty people killed when the Rome and Vienna airports were bombed, and then in April 1986 another bomb exploded in a discotheque in West Berlin that was a hangout for American servicemen. U.S. intelligence tied Libya to both of these bombings, and the eventual outcome was an American air attack in which one of the residences of Qaddafi was hit.

In retaliation, the Palestinian terrorist Abu Nidal executed three U.S. citizens who worked at the American University in Beirut. But Qaddafi himself—no doubt surprised and shaken by the American reprisal—went into a brief period of retirement as a sponsor of terrorism. So far as we know, it took nearly three years (until December 1988) before he could pull himself together to the point of undertaking another operation: the bombing of Pan Am flight 103 over Lockerbie, Scotland, in which 270 people lost their lives. Of the two Libyan intelligence agents who were tried in a Scottish court for planting the bomb, one was convicted (though not until 2001) and the other acquitted. Qaddafi himself suffered no further punishment from American warplanes.

In January 1989, Reagan was succeeded by the first George Bush, who, in handling the fallout from the destruction of Pan Am 103, was content to adopt the approach to terrorism taken by all his predecessors. During the elder Bush's four-year period in the White House, there were several attacks on Americans in Turkey by Islamic terrorist organizations, and there were others in Egypt, Saudi Arabia, and Lebanon. None of these was as bloody as previous incidents, and none provoked any military response from the United States.

In January 1993, Bill Clinton became president. Over the span of his two terms in office, American citizens continued to be injured or killed in Israel and other countries by terrorists who were not aiming specifically at the United States. But the United States was most emphatically the target of several sensational terrorist operations that occurred on Clinton's watch.

The first, on February 26, 1993, only thirty-eight days after his inauguration, was the explosion of a truck bomb in the parking garage of the World Trade Center. As compared with what would happen to the same buildings on September 11, 2001, this was a minor incident in which "only" six people were killed and over one thousand injured. Eventually, the mastermind of the operation, the blind sheik Omar Abdel Rahman, and ten other radical Islamists (including Ramzi Yousef, the most important of them) were caught, tried, convicted, and sent to prison for long terms.

But in following the by-now traditional pattern and treating the attack as either a common crime or the work of a rogue group acting on its own, the Clinton administration willfully turned a deaf ear to outside experts like Steven Emerson and even its own CIA director, R. James Woolsey, who strongly suspected that behind the individual culprits was a terrorist Islamic network with (at that time) its headquarters in Sudan. This network, then scarcely known to the general public, was called Al Qaeda, and its leader was a former Saudi national who had fought on our side against the Soviets in Afghanistan but had since turned against us as fiercely as he had been against the Russians.

His name was Osama bin Laden.

The next major episode was not long in trailing the bombing of the World Trade Center. In April 1993, less than two months after that attack, former President Bush visited Kuwait, where an attempt was made to assassinate him by—as our own investigators were able to determine—Iraqi intelligence agents. The Clinton administration spent two more months seeking approval from the UN and the "international community" to retaliate for this egregious assault on the United States. In the end, a few cruise missiles were fired into the Iraqi capital of Baghdad, where they fell harmlessly onto empty buildings in the middle of the night.

In the years immediately ahead, there were many Islamic terrorist operations (in Turkey, Pakistan, Saudi Arabia, Lebanon, Yemen, and Israel) that were not specifically aimed at the United States but in which Americans were nevertheless murdered or kidnapped. In March 1995, however, a van belonging to the U.S. consulate in Karachi, Pakistan, was hit by gunfire, killing two American diplomats and injuring a third. In November of the same year, five Americans died when a car bomb exploded in Riyadh, Saudi Arabia, near a building in which a U.S. military advisory group lived.

All this was trumped in June 1996 when another building in which American military personnel lived—the Khobar Towers in Dhahran, Saudi Arabia—was blasted by a truck bomb. Nineteen of our airmen were killed, and 240 other Americans on the premises were wounded.

In 1993 Clinton had been so intent on treating the World Trade Center bombing as a common crime that for some time afterward he refused even to meet with his own CIA director. Perhaps he anticipated that he would be told things by Woolsey— about terrorist networks and the states sponsoring them—that he did not wish to hear, because he had no intention of embarking on the military action that such knowledge might force upon him.

Now, in the wake of the bombing of the Khobar Towers, Clinton again handed the matter over to the police, but the man in charge, his FBI director, Louis Freeh, who had intimations of an Iranian connection, could no more get through to him than Woolsey before. There were a few arrests, and the action then duly moved into the courts.

In June 1998 grenades were unsuccessfully hurled at the U.S. embassy in Beirut. A little later, our embassies in the capitals of Kenya (Nairobi) and Tanzania (Dar es Salaam) were not so lucky. On a single day—August 7, 1998—car bombs went off in both places, leaving more than two hundred people dead, of whom twelve were Americans. Credit for this coordinated operation was claimed by Al Qaeda. In what, whether fairly or not, was widely interpreted, especially abroad, as a move to distract attention from his legal troubles over the Monica Lewinsky affair, Clinton fired cruise missiles at an Al Qaeda training camp in Afghanistan, where bin Laden was supposed to be at that moment, and at a building in Sudan, where Al Qaeda also had a base. But bin Laden escaped harm, while it remained uncertain whether a targeted factory in Sudan was actually manufacturing chemical weapons or was just a normal pharmaceutical plant.

This fiasco—so we have learned from former members of his administration—discouraged any further such action by Clinton against bin Laden, though we have also learned from various sources that he did authorize a number of covert counterterrorist operations and diplomatic initiatives leading to arrests in foreign countries. But according to Dick Morris, who was then Clinton's political adviser:

> The weekly strategy meetings at the White House throughout 1995 and 1996 featured an escalating drumbeat of advice to President Clinton to take decisive steps to crack down on terrorism. The polls gave these ideas a green light. But Clinton hesitated and failed to act, always finding a reason why some other concern was more important.

In the period after Morris left, more began going on behind the scenes, but most of it remained in the realm of talk or planning that went nowhere. In contrast to the flattering picture of Clinton that Richard Clarke would subsequently draw, Woolsey (who after a brief tenure resigned from the CIA out of sheer frustration) would offer a devastating retrospective summary of the president's overall approach:

> Do something to show you're concerned. Launch a few missiles in the desert, bop them on the head, arrest a few people. But just keep kicking the ball down field.

Bin Laden, picking up that ball on October 12, 2000, when the USS *Cole* docked for refueling in Yemen, dispatched a small boat carrying a team of suicide bombers. The bombers did not succeed in sinking the ship, but they inflicted severe damage upon it, while managing to kill seventeen American sailors and wound another thirty-nine. This was enough, and more than enough, to satisfy bin Laden. As Michael Dobbs of the *Washington Post* would later report:

> In a video that circulated widely in the Arab world . . . [bin Laden] bragged of the attack on the USS Cole. . . . The destroyer had the "illusion that she could destroy anything," but was itself destroyed by a tiny boat. . . . "The destroyer represented the West and the small boat represented Muhammad," he boasted.

At the time of the attack on the *Cole*, bin Laden had not yet taken credit for it, but Clarke, along with a few intelligence analysts, had no doubt that the culprit was Al Qaeda. The heads of neither the CIA nor the FBI, however, thought the case was conclusive. Hence, the United States did not so much as lift a military finger against bin Laden or the Taliban regime in Afghanistan, where he was now ensconced and being protected. As for Clinton, so obsessively was he then wrapped up in a futile attempt to broker a deal between the Israelis and the Palestinians that all he could see in this attack on an American warship was an effort "to deter us from our mission of promoting peace and security in the Middle East." The terrorists, he resoundingly vowed, would "fail utterly" in this objective.

Never mind that not the slightest indication existed that bin Laden was in the least concerned over Clinton's negotiations with the Israelis and the Palestinians at Camp David, or even that the Palestinian issue was of primary importance to him as compared with other grievances. His own Palestinian mentor, Abdullah Azzam, had declared that the liberation of Palestine had to wait upon the liberation of Afghanistan, while his deputy Ayman al-Zawahiri had written an article entitled "The Way to Jerusalem Passes Through Cairo," in which he argued that the overthrow of secular Arab regimes such as the one in Egypt took precedence over the struggle against Israel. As for bin Laden himself, he had already made clear in various public statements that the Palestinians came in only third in his list of grievances. They lagged behind the "occupation" of Saudi Arabia by American "crusader forces" ("their filthy feet roaming everywhere" in "the land of the two holy places"—that is, Mecca and Medina) and the "starving" of the children of Iraq through the sanctions that had been imposed on Saddam Hussein after the first Gulf War of 1991 (long before, be it noted, the American invasion of 2003). And in the Al Qaeda training camps, where the recruits in an ideology class were given a list of the main enemies of Islam, Israel ranked only fourth, trailing "Heretics (the Mubaraks of the world), Shiites, and America."

In any event, it was Clinton who failed, not bin Laden. The Palestinians under Yasir Arafat, spurning an unprecedentedly generous offer that had been made by the Israeli prime minister, Ehud Barak, with Clinton's enthusiastic endorsement, unleashed a new round of terrorism. And bin Laden, who had told an American journalist back in 1998 that the war he was fighting would "inevitably move . . . to American soil," would soon succeed all too well in making good on this brazen promise.

The sheer audacity of what bin Laden went on to do on September 11 was unquestionably a product of his contempt for American power. Our persistent refusal for so long to use that power against him and his terrorist brethren—or to do so effectively whenever we tried—reinforced his conviction that we were a nation on the way down, destined to be defeated by the resurgence of the same Islamic militancy that had once conquered and converted large parts of the world by the sword.

As bin Laden saw it, thousands or even millions of his followers and sympathizers all over the Muslim world were willing, and even eager, to die a martyr's death in the *jihad*, the holy war, against the "Great Satan," as the Ayatollah Khomeini had called us. But, in bin Laden's view, we in the West, and especially in America, were all so afraid to die that we lacked the will even to stand up for ourselves and defend our degenerate way of life.

Bin Laden was never reticent or coy in laying out this assessment of the United States. In an interview on CNN in 1997, he declared that "the myth of the superpower was destroyed not only in my mind but also in the minds of all Muslims" when the Soviet Union was defeated in Afghanistan. That the Muslim fighters in Afghanistan would almost certainly have failed if not for the arms supplied to them by the United States under Ronald Reagan did not seem to enter into the lesson he drew from the Soviet defeat. On the contrary: in an interview a year earlier, he belittled the United States as compared with the Soviet Union. "The Russian soldier is more courageous and patient than the U.S. soldier," he said. Hence, "our battle with the United States is easy compared with the battles in which we engaged in Afghanistan."

Becoming still more explicit, he wrote off the Americans as cowards. Had Reagan not taken to his heels in Lebanon after the bombing of the Marine barracks in 1983? And had not Clinton done the same a decade later when only a few American Rangers were killed in Somalia, where they had been sent to participate in a "peacekeeping" mission? Bin Laden did not boast of this as one of his victories, but a State Department dossier charged that Al Qaeda had trained the terrorists who ambushed the American servicemen. (The ugly story of what happened to us in Somalia was told in the film version of Mark Bowden's *Black Hawk Down*, which reportedly became Saddam Hussein's favorite movie.)

Bin Laden summed it all up in a third interview he gave in 1998:

> After leaving Afghanistan the Muslim fighters headed for Somalia and prepared for a long battle thinking that the Americans were like the Russians. The youth were surprised at the low morale of the American soldiers and realized, more than before, that the American soldier was a paper tiger and after a few blows ran in defeat.

Bin Laden was not the first enemy of a democratic regime to have been emboldened by such impressions. In the 1930s, Adolf Hitler was convinced both by the failure of the British to arm themselves against the threat he posed and by the policy of appeasement they adopted toward him that they were decadent and would never fight no matter how many countries he invaded.

Similarly with Joseph Stalin in the immediate aftermath of World War II. Encouraged by the rapid demobilization of the United States, which to him meant that we were unprepared and unwilling to resist him with military force, Stalin broke the pledges he had made at Yalta to hold free elections in the countries of Eastern Europe he had occupied at the end of the war. Instead, he consolidated his hold over those countries and made menacing gestures toward Greece and Turkey.

After Stalin's death, his successors repeatedly played the same game whenever they sensed a weakening of the American resolve to hold them back. Sometimes this took the form of maneuvers aimed at establishing a balance of military power in their favor. Sometimes it took the form of using local Communist parties or other proxies as their instrument. But thanks to the decline of American power following our withdrawal from Vietnam—a decline reflected in the spread during the late 1970s of isolationist and pacifist sentiment, which was in turn reflected in severely reduced military spending—Leonid Brezhnev felt safe in sending his own troops into Afghanistan in 1979.

It was the same decline of American power, so uncannily personified by Jimmy Carter, that, less than two months before the Soviet invasion of Afghanistan, had emboldened the Ayatollah Khomeini to seize and hold American hostages. To be sure, there were those who denied that this daring action had anything to do with Khomeini's belief that the United States under Carter had become impotent. But this denial was impossible to sustain in the face of the contrast between the attack on our embassy in Tehran and the protection the Khomeini regime extended to the Soviet embassy there when a group of protesters tried to storm it after the invasion of Afghanistan. The radical Muslim fundamentalists ruling Iran hated communism and the Soviet Union at least as much as they hated us—especially now that the Soviets had invaded a Muslim country. Therefore, the difference in Khomeini's treatment of the two embassies could not be explained by ideological or political factors. What could and did explain it was his fear of Soviet retaliation as against his expectation that the United States, having lost its nerve, would go to any lengths to avoid the use of force.

And so it was with Saddam Hussein. In 1990, with the first George Bush sitting in the White House, Saddam Hussein invaded Kuwait in what was widely, and accurately, seen as a first step in a bid to seize control of the oil fields of the Middle East. The elder Bush, fortified by the determination of Margaret Thatcher, who was then prime minister of England, declared that the invasion would not stand, and he put together a coalition that prepared itself to send a great military force into the region. This alone might well have frightened Saddam Hussein into pulling out of Kuwait if not for the wave of hysteria in the United States about the tens of thousands of "body bags" that it was predicted would be flown home if we actually went to war with Iraq. Not unreasonably, Saddam concluded that, if he held firm, it was we who would blink and back down.

The fact that Saddam miscalculated, and that in the end we

made good on our threat, did not overly impress Osama bin Laden. After all, dreading the casualties we would suffer if we went into Baghdad after liberating Kuwait and defeating the Iraqi army on the battlefield, we had allowed Saddam to remain in power. To bin Laden, this could only have looked like further evidence of the weakness we had shown in the ineffectual policy toward terrorism adopted by a long string of American presidents. No wonder he was persuaded that he could strike us massively on our own soil and get away with it.

Yet just as Saddam had miscalculated in 1990–91, and would again in 2002, bin Laden misread how the Americans would react to being hit where, literally, they lived. In all likelihood, he expected a collapse into despair and demoralization; what he elicited instead was an outpouring of rage and an upsurge of patriotic sentiment such as younger Americans had never witnessed except in the movies and had most assuredly never experienced in their own hearts and souls, or, for those who enlisted in the military, in their own flesh.

In that sense, bin Laden did for this country what the Ayatollah Khomeini had done before him. In seizing the American hostages in 1979 and escaping retaliation, Khomeini inflicted a great humiliation on the United States. But at the same time, he also exposed the foolishness of Jimmy Carter's view of the world. The foolishness did not lie in the recognition that American power—military, economic, political, and moral—had been on a steep decline at least since Vietnam. This was all too true. What was foolish was the conclusion Carter drew from it. Rather than proposing policies aimed at halting and then reversing the decline, he took the position that the cause was the play of historical forces we could do nothing to stop or even slow down. Instead of complaining or flailing about in a vain and dangerous effort to recapture our lost place in the sun, said Carter, we needed first to acknowledge, accept, and adjust to this inexorable historical development, and then to act upon it with "mature restraint."

In one fell swoop, the Ayatollah Khomeini made nonsense of

Carter's delusionary philosophy in the eyes of very large numbers of Americans, including many who had previously entertained it. Correlatively, new heart was given to those who, rejecting the idea that American decline was inevitable, had argued that the cause was bad policies and that the decline could be turned around by returning to the better policies that had made us so powerful in the first place.

The entire episode thereby became one of the forces behind an already burgeoning determination to rebuild American power that culminated in the election of Ronald Reagan, who had campaigned on the promise to do just that. For all the shortcomings of his own handling of terrorism, Reagan did in fact keep his promise to rebuild American power. And it was this that set the stage for victory in World War III—the multifaceted war we had been waging since 1947, when the United States under President Harry Truman, aroused by Stalin's miscalculation, decided to resist any further advance of the Soviet empire.

Few, if any, of Harry Truman's contemporaries would have dreamed that this product of a Kansas City political machine, who as a reputedly run-of-the-mill U.S. senator had spent most of his time on taxes and railroads, would rise so resolutely and so brilliantly to the threat represented by Soviet imperialism. Just so, fifty-four years later in 2001, another politician with a small reputation and little previous interest in foreign affairs would be confronted with a challenge perhaps even greater than the one faced by Harry Truman, and he too astonished his own contemporaries by the way he rose to it.

CHAPTER THREE

ENTER THE BUSH DOCTRINE

I N "The Sources of Soviet Conduct" (1947), the theoretical defense he constructed of the strategy Truman would adopt for fighting the war ahead, George F. Kennan, then the director of the State Department's policy planning staff, and writing under the pseudonym "X," described that strategy as

> a long-term, patient but firm and vigilant containment of Russian expansive tendencies . . . by the adroit and vigilant application of counterforce at a series of constantly shifting georgraphical and political points.

In other words (though Kennan himself did not use those words), we were faced with the prospect of nothing less than another world war; and (though in later years, against the plain sense of the words that he himself did use, Kennan tried to claim that the "counterforce" he had in mind was only political and economic) this new world war would not, as calling it the cold war misleadingly suggested, lack for hot military engagements. Before it was over, close to 100,000 Americans would die on the far-off battlefields of Korea and Vietnam, and the blood of many others allied with us in the political and ideological struggle against the Soviet Union would be spilled on those same battlefields, and in many other places as well.

So we can add these hot episodes to the reasons I have already given for believing that the cold war is a misleading name and should from now on be recognized as World War III. And to the key features that Eliot Cohen said World War IV shares with World War III (a mixture of violent and nonviolent efforts instead of multimillion-man armies and conventional front lines; a duration measured in decades rather than years; and deep ideological roots), I would add one more that Cohen did not mention: both World War III and World War IV were declared through the enunciation of presidential doctrines.

The Truman Doctrine of 1947 was born with the announcement that "it must be the policy of the United States to support free peoples who are resisting attempted subjugation by armed minorities or by outside pressure." Beginning with a special program of aid to Greece and Turkey, which were then threatened by Communist takeovers, the strategy was broadened within a few months by the launching of a much larger and more significant program of economic aid that came to be called the Marshall Plan. The purpose of the Marshall Plan was to hasten the reconstruction of the war-torn economies of Western Europe—not only because this was a good thing in itself, and not only because it would serve American interests, but also because it could help eliminate the grievances on which it was thought that communism fed. But then came a Communist coup in Czechoslovakia. Following as it had upon the installation by the Soviet Union of puppet regimes in the occupied countries of Eastern Europe, the Czech coup demonstrated that economic measures would not be enough by themselves to ward off a comparable danger posed to Italy and France by huge local Communist parties entirely subservient to Moscow. Out of this realization—and out of a parallel worry about an actual Soviet invasion of Western Europe—came the North Atlantic Treaty Organization (NATO).

Containment, then, was a three-sided strategy made up of economic, political, and military components. All three would be deployed in a shifting relative balance over the four decades it took to win World War III (twenty-seven years more than Kennan thought would be required for the strategy to achieve its objective in the "implosion" of the Soviet Union).

If the Truman Doctrine unfolded gradually, revealing its entire meaning only in stages, the Bush Doctrine was pretty fully enunciated in a single speech, delivered to a joint session of Congress on September 20, 2001. It was then clarified and elaborated in three subsequent statements: Bush's first State of the Union address on January 29, 2002; his speech to the graduating class of the U.S. Military Academy at West Point on June 1, 2002; and the remarks he made at the White House on June 24, 2002. This difference aside, Bush's contemporaries were at least as startled as Truman's had been, both by the substance of the new doctrine and by the transformation it bespoke in its author. For here was George W. Bush, who in foreign affairs had been a more or less passive disciple of his father, talking for all the world like a fiery follower of Ronald Reagan.

In sharp contrast to Reagan, who was generally considered a dangerous ideologue, George H. W. Bush—who had been Reagan's vice president and had then succeeded him in the White House—was often accused of being deficient in what he himself inelegantly dismissed as "the vision thing." The charge was fair in that the elder Bush had no guiding sense of the role the United States might play in reshaping the post–cold war world. A strong adherent of the "realist" perspective on world affairs, he believed that the maintenance of stability was the proper purpose of American foreign policy, and the only wise and prudential course to follow. Therefore, when Saddam Hussein upset the balance of power in the Middle East by invading Kuwait in 1991, the elder Bush went to war not to create a new configuration in the region but to restore the status quo ante. And it was precisely out of the same overriding concern for stability that, having achieved this objective by driving Saddam out of Kuwait, Bush then allowed him to remain in power.

As for the second President Bush, before 9/11 he was, to all appearances, as deficient in the "vision thing" as his father before him. If he entertained any doubts about the soundness of the realist approach, he showed no sign of it. Nothing he said or did gave any indication that he might be dissatisfied with the idea that his main job in foreign affairs was to keep things on an even keel. Nor was there any visible indication that he might be drawn to Ronald Reagan's more "idealistic" ambition to change the world, especially with the "Wilsonian" aim of making it "safe for democracy" by encouraging the spread to as many other countries as possible of the liberties we Americans enjoyed.

Which was why Bush's address of September 20, 2001, came as so great a surprise. Delivered only nine days after the attacks on the World Trade Center and the Pentagon, and officially declaring that the United States was now at war, the September 20 speech put this nation, and all others, on notice that, whether or not George W. Bush had been a strictly conventional realist in the mold of his father, he was now politically born again as a passionate democratic idealist of the Reaganite stamp.

It was also this speech that marked the emergence of the Bush Doctrine and pointed just as clearly to World War IV as the Truman Doctrine had to World War III. As I indicated in the Prologue, Bush did not explicitly give the name World War IV to the struggle ahead against the "global terrorist network" that had attacked us on our own soil, but he did characterize it as a direct successor to the two world wars that had immediately preceded it. Even though I have already quoted the relevant passage, it is so important to an understanding of the Bush Doctrine that I want to quote it again:

> We have seen their kind before. They're the heirs of all the murderous ideologies of the twentieth century. By sacrificing human life to serve their radical visions, by abandoning every value except the will to power, they follow in the path of fascism, Nazism, and totalitarianism. And they will follow that path all the way to where it ends in history's unmarked grave of discarded lies.

As this passage, coming toward the beginning of the speech, linked the Bush Doctrine to the Truman Doctrine and to the great struggle led by Franklin D. Roosevelt before it, the wind-up section demonstrated that if the second President Bush had previously lacked "the vision thing," his eyes were blazing with it now. "Great harm has been done to us," he intoned toward the end. "We have suffered great loss. And in our grief and anger we have found our mission and our moment." Then he went on to spell out the substance of that mission and that moment:

> The advance of human freedom, the great achievement of our time and the great hope of every time, now depends on us. Our nation, this generation, will lift the dark threat of violence from our people and our future. We will rally the world to this cause by our efforts, by our courage. We will not tire, we will not falter, and we will not fail.

Finally, in his peroration, drawing on some of the same language he had been applying to the nation as a whole, Bush shifted into the first person, pledging his own commitment to the great mission we were all charged with accomplishing:

> I will not forget the wound to our country and those who inflicted it. I will not yield, I will not rest, I will not relent in waging this struggle for freedom and security for the American people. The course of this conflict is not known, yet its outcome is certain. Freedom and fear, justice and cruelty, have always been at war, and we know that God is not neutral between them.

Not even Ronald Reagan, the "Great Communicator" himself, had ever been so eloquent in expressing the "idealistic" impetus behind his conception of the American role in the world.*

* In expressing his determination to win the war, however, Bush was mainly reaching back to the language of Winston Churchill, who vowed as World War II was getting under way in 1940: "We shall not flag or fail. We shall go on to the end."

This was not the last time Bush would sound these themes. Two and a half years later, at a moment when things seemed to be going badly in the war, it was with the same ideas he had originally put forward on September 20, 2001, that he sought to reassure the nation. The occasion would be a commencement address at the Air Force Academy on June 2, 2004, where he would once again, and repeatedly, place the "war against terrorism" in direct succession to World War II and World War III. He would also be unusually undiplomatic in making no bones about his rejection of realism:

> For decades, free nations tolerated oppression in the Middle East for the sake of stability. In practice, this approach brought little stability and much oppression, so I have changed this policy.

And again, even less diplomatically:

> Some who call themselves realists question whether the spread of democracy in the Middle East should be any concern of ours. But the realists in this case have lost contact with a fundamental reality: America has always been less secure when freedom is in retreat; America is always more secure when freedom is on the march.

To top it all off, he would go out of his way to assert that his own policy, which he properly justified in the first place as a better way to protect American interests than the alternative favored by the realists, also bore the stamp of the Reaganite version of Wilsonian idealism:

> This conflict will take many turns with setbacks on the course to victory. Through it all, our confidence comes from one unshakable belief: we believe in Ronald Reagan's words that "the future belongs to the free."

The first pillar of the Bush Doctrine, then, was built on a repudiation of moral relativism, an entirely unapologetic assertion of the need for and the possibility of moral judgment in the realm of world affairs, and a correlative determination to foster "the spread of democracy in the Middle East." And just to make sure that the point he had first made on September 20, 2001, had hit home, Bush returned to it even more outspokenly and in greater detail in the State of the Union address of January 29, 2002.

Bush had won enthusiastic plaudits from many for the "moral clarity" of his September 20 speech, but his "simplistic" ideas had also provoked even greater dismay and disgust among "advanced" thinkers and "sophisticated" commentators and diplomats both at home and abroad. Now he intensified and exacerbated their outrage by becoming more specific. Having spoken in September only in general terms about the enemy in World War IV, Bush proceeded in his second major wartime pronouncement to single out three such nations—Iraq, Iran, and North Korea—which he described as forming an "axis of evil."

Here again he was following in the footsteps of Ronald Reagan, who had denounced the Soviet Union, our principal enemy in World War III, as an "evil empire," and who had been answered with a veritably hysterical outcry from chancelleries and campuses and editorial pages all over the world. Evil? What place did a word like that have in the lexicon of international affairs, assuming it would ever occur to an enlightened person to exhume it from the grave of obsolete concepts in any connection whatsoever? But in the eyes of the "experts," Reagan was not an enlightened person. Instead, he was a "cowboy," a B-movie actor, who had by some freak of democratic perversity landed in the White House. In denouncing the Soviet empire, he was accused either of signaling an intention to trigger a nuclear war or of being too stupid to understand that his wildly provocative rhetoric might do so inadvertently.

The reaction to Bush was perhaps less hysterical and more scornful than the outcry against Reagan, since this time there was no carrying-on about a nuclear war. But the air was just as thick with the old sneers and jeers. Who but an ignoramus and a simpleton—or a fanatical religious fundamentalist, of the very type on whom Bush was declaring war—would resort to archaic moral absolutes like "good" and "evil"? On the one hand, it was egregiously simple-minded to brand a whole nation as evil, and on the other, only a fool could bring himself to believe, as Bush (once more like Reagan) had evidently done in complete and ingenuous sincerity, that the United States, of all countries, represented the good. Surely only a know-nothing illiterate could be oblivious to the innumerable crimes committed by America both at home and abroad—crimes that the country's own leading intellectuals had so richly documented in the by-now-standard academic view of its history.

Here was how Gore Vidal, one of those intellectuals, stated the case:

> I mean, to watch Bush doing his little war dance in Congress . . . about "evildoers" and this "axis of evil" . . . I thought, he doesn't even know what the word *axis* means. Somebody just gave it to him. . . . This is about as mindless a statement as you could make. Then he comes up with about a dozen other countries that have "evil" people in them, who might commit "terrorist acts." What is a terrorist act? Whatever he thinks is a terrorist act. And we are going to go after them. Because we are good and they are evil. And we're "gonna git 'em."

This was rougher and cruder than the language issuing from editorial pages and think tanks and foreign ministries and even most other intellectuals, but it was no different from what nearly all of them thought and how many of them talked in private. And yet Churchill, who had been the target of many derogatory epithets in his long career but who was never regarded even by his worst enemies as "simple-minded," had no hesitation in attaching a phrase like "monster of wickedness" to Hitler, which he did in 1941, even before he or anyone else knew the full extent of the evils the Nazis were about to commit. Nor did the political philosopher Hannah Arendt, whose mind was, if anything, over-complicated rather than too simple, have any problem in her masterpiece, *The Origins of Totalitarianism*, with calling both Nazism and communism "absolute evil."

As soon became clear, however, Bush was not deterred. In subsequent statements he continued to uphold the first pillar of his new doctrine and to affirm the universality of the moral purposes animating this new war:

> Some worry that it is somehow undiplomatic or impolite to speak the language of right and wrong. I disagree. Different circumstances require different methods, but not different moralities. Moral truth is the same in every culture, in every time, and in every place. . . . We are in a conflict between good and evil, and America will call evil by its name.

Then, in a fascinating leap into the great theoretical debate of the post–cold war era (though without identifying the main participants), Bush came down squarely on the side of Francis Fukuyama's much-misunderstood view of "the end of history," according to which the demise of communism had eliminated the only serious competitor to our own political system. Bush:

> The twentieth century ended with a single surviving model of human progress, based on non-negotiable demands of human dignity, the rule of law, limits on the power of the state, respect for women and private property and free speech and equal justice and religious tolerance.

Having endorsed Fukuyama (who did not return the compliment and would later emerge as a stern critic of the Bush Doctrine), the president now brushed off the rival theory, developed most fully by Samuel Huntington of Harvard, which postulated a "clash of civilizations" arising from the supposedly incompatible values prevailing in different parts of the world. Bush again:

When it comes to the common rights and needs of men and women, there is no clash of civilizations. The requirements of freedom apply fully to Africa and Latin America and the entire Islamic world. The peoples of the Islamic nations want and deserve the same freedoms and opportunities as people in every nation. And their governments should listen to their hopes.

As we shall see, Bush would hold fast to this conviction through thick and thin, and in spite of the many signs to which his critics would point as evidence to the contrary.

If, then, the first of the three pillars on which the Bush Doctrine stood was a new moral attitude with powerful political implications, the second was a comparably dramatic shift, carrying equally consequential political implications, in the conception of terrorism as it had come to be defined in standard academic and intellectual discourse.

Under this new understanding—confirmed over and over again by the fact that most of the terrorists about whom we were learning came from prosperous families—terrorism was no longer considered a product of economic factors. The "swamps" out of which this murderous plague grew were the outcome not, as the old understanding had held, of poverty and hunger but of political oppression. It was only by "draining" those swamps, through a strategy of "regime change," that we would be making ourselves safe from the threat of terrorism and simultaneously giving the peoples of "the entire Islamic world" the freedoms "they want and deserve."

In the new understanding, furthermore, terrorists, with rare exceptions, were not individual psychotics acting on their own; they were, rather, agents of organizations that depended on the sponsorship of various governments. Our aim, therefore, could not be merely to capture or kill Osama bin Laden and wipe out the Al Qaeda terrorists under his direct leadership. Bush declared that we would also need to uproot and destroy the entire network of interconnected terrorist organizations and cells "with global reach" that existed in as many as fifty or sixty countries. No longer could we treat the members of these groups as criminals to be arrested by the police, read their Miranda rights, and brought to trial. From now on, they were to be regarded as the irregular troops of a military alliance at war with the United States, and indeed the civilized world as a whole.

Not that this analysis of terrorism had exactly been a secret. The State Department itself had a list of seven state sponsors of terrorism (all but two of which, Cuba and North Korea, were predominantly Muslim), and it regularly issued reports on terrorist incidents throughout the world. But aside from such actions as the lobbing of a cruise missile or two, diplomatic and/or economic sanctions that were inconsistently and even perfunctorily enforced, and a number of covert operations, the law enforcement approach still prevailed.

September 11 changed much—if not yet all—of that. Still in use were atavistic phrases like "bringing the terrorists to justice," but no one could any longer dream that the American answer to what had been done to us in New York and Washington would begin with an FBI investigation and end with a series of ordinary criminal trials. War had been declared on the United States, and to war we were going to go.

But against whom? Since it was certain that Osama bin Laden had masterminded September 11, and since he and the top leadership of Al Qaeda were holed up in Afghanistan, the first target, and thus the first testing ground of this second pillar of the Bush Doctrine, chose itself.

Before resorting to military force, however, Bush issued an ultimatum to the extreme Islamic fundamentalists of the Taliban who were then ruling Afghanistan (and who represented the main religious face of the two-headed monster I have been calling Islamofascism). The ultimatum demanded that they turn Osama bin Laden and his people over to us and that they shut down all terrorist training camps there. By rejecting this ultimatum, the Taliban not only asked for an invasion but, under the Bush

Doctrine, also asked to be overthrown. And so, on October 7, 2001, the United States—joined by Great Britain and about a dozen other countries—launched a military campaign against both Al Qaeda and the regime that was providing it with "aid and safe haven."

As compared with what would come later, there was relatively little opposition either at home or abroad to the opening of this first front of World War IV. The reason was that the Afghan campaign could easily be justified as a retaliatory strike against the terrorists who had attacked us. And while there was a good deal of murmuring against the dangers of pursuing a policy of "regime change," there was very little sympathy in practice (outside the Muslim world, that is) for the Taliban.

Whatever domestic opposition was mounted against the Afghanistan campaign mainly took the form of skepticism over the chances of winning it. True, such skepticism was in some quarters a mask for outright opposition to American military power in general. But once the invasion got under way, the main focus shifted to everything that seemed to be going awry on the battlefield.

For example, only a couple of weeks into the campaign, when there were missteps involving the use of the Afghan fighters of the Northern Alliance, observers like R. W. Apple of the *New York Times* immediately rushed to conjure up the ghost of Vietnam. This restless spirit, having been called forth from the vasty deep, henceforth refused to be exorcised, and would go on to elbow its way into every detail of all the debates to come over World War IV. On this occasion, its message was that we were falling victim to the illusion that we could rely on an incompetent local force to do the fighting on the ground while we supplied advice and air support. This strategy would inevitably fail, and would suck us into the same "quagmire" into which we had been dragged in Vietnam. After all, as Apple and others argued, the Soviet Union had suffered its own "Vietnam" in Afghanistan—and unlike us, it had not been hampered by the logistical problems of projecting power over a great distance. How could we expect to do better?

When, however, the B-52's and the 15,000-pound "Daisy Cutter" bombs were unleashed, they temporarily banished the ghost of Vietnam and undercut the fears of some (and the hopes of others) that we were heading into a quagmire. Far from being good for nothing but "pounding the rubble," as the critics had sarcastically charged, the Daisy Cutters exerted, as even a *New York Times* report was forced to concede, "a terrifying psychological impact as they exploded just above ground, wiping out everything for hundreds of yards."

But the Daisy Cutters were only the half of it. As we were all to discover, our "smart-bomb" technology had advanced far beyond the stage it had reached when first introduced in 1991. In Afghanistan in 2001, such bombs—guided by "spotters" on the ground who often rode on horseback, were equipped with radios, laptops, and lasers, and were also aided by unmanned satellite drones and other systems in the air—proved to be both incredibly precise in avoiding civilian casualties and absolutely lethal in destroying the enemy. It was this "new kind of American power," added the *New York Times* report, that "enabled a ragtag opposition" (i.e., the same Northern Alliance supposedly dragging us into a quagmire) to rout the "battle-hardened troops" of the Taliban regime in less than three months, and with the loss of very few American lives.

In the event, Osama bin Laden was not captured and Al Qaeda was not totally destroyed. But it was certainly damaged by the campaign in Afghanistan. As for the Taliban regime, it was overthrown and replaced by a government that would no longer give aid and comfort to terrorists. Moreover, while Afghanistan under the new government may not have been exactly democratic, it was infinitely less oppressive than its totalitarian predecessor. And thanks to the clearing of political ground that had been covered over by the radical Islamic fundamentalism of the Taliban, the seeds of free institutions were being sown and given a chance to sprout and grow.

The campaign in Afghanistan demonstrated in the most unambiguous terms what followed from the new understanding of terrorism that formed the second pillar of the Bush Doctrine: countries that gave safe haven to terrorists and refused to clean them out were asking the United States to do it for them, and the regimes ruling these countries were also asking to be overthrown in favor of new leaders with democratic aspirations. Of course, as circumstances permitted and prudence dictated, other instruments of power, whether economic or diplomatic, would be deployed. But Afghanistan showed that the military option was open, available for use, and lethally effective.

So too with the second front of World War IV that the United States would soon open in Iraq. But if Afghanistan was invaded under the aegis of the new understanding of terrorism enunciated by the second pillar of the Bush Doctrine, it was the third pillar on which the Bush Doctrine stood—the assertion of our right to preempt—that would dictate the invasion of Iraq.

Bush had already pretty clearly indicated on September 20, 2001, that he had no intention of waiting around to be attacked again ("we will pursue nations that provide aid or safe haven to terrorism"). But in the State of the Union speech of January 29, 2002, he became much more explicit on this point:

> We'll be deliberate, yet time is not on our side. I will not wait on events, while dangers gather. I will not stand by, as peril draws closer and closer. The United States of America will not permit the world's most dangerous regimes to threaten us with the world's most destructive weapons.

To those with ears to hear, the January speech should have made it abundantly clear that Bush was now proposing to go beyond the fundamentally retaliatory strike against Afghanistan and to take preemptive action. Yet at first it went largely unnoticed that this right to strike, not in retaliation for but in anticipation of an attack, was a logical extension of the general outline Bush had provided on September 20. Nor did the new position attract much attention even when it was reiterated in the plainest of words on January 29. It was not until the third in the series of major speeches elaborating on the Bush Doctrine—the one delivered on June 1, 2002, at West Point to the graduating class of newly commissioned officers of the United States Army—that the message got through at last.

Perhaps the reason the preemption pillar finally became clearly visible at West Point was that, for the first time, Bush placed his new ideas in historical context:

> For much of the last century, America's defense relied on the cold war doctrines of deterrence and containment. In some cases, those strategies still apply. But new threats also require new thinking. Deterrence—the promise of massive retaliation against nations— means nothing against shadowy terrorist networks with no nation or citizens to defend.

This covered Al Qaeda and similar groups. But Bush then proceeded to explain, in addition, why the old doctrines could not work with a regime like Saddam Hussein's in Iraq:

> Containment is not possible when unbalanced dictators with weapons of mass destruction can deliver those weapons or missiles or secretly provide them to terrorist allies.

Refusing to flinch from the implications of this analysis, Bush repudiated the previously sacred dogmas of arms control and treaties against the proliferation of weapons of mass destruction as a means of dealing with the dangers now facing us from Iraq and other members of the axis of evil:

> We cannot defend America and our friends by hoping for the best. We cannot put our faith in the word of tyrants, who solemnly sign nonproliferation treaties, and then systematically break them.

Hence, Bush inexorably continued,

> If we wait for threats to fully materialize, we will have waited too
> long. . . . The war on terror will not be won on the defensive. We
> must take the battle to the enemy, disrupt his plans, and confront
> the worst threats before they emerge. In the world we have en-
> tered, the only path to safety is the path of action. And this na-
> tion will act.

At this early stage, the Bush administration was still denying
that it had reached any definite decision about Saddam Hussein,
but everyone knew that, in promising to act, Bush was talking
about him. The immediate purpose was to topple the Iraqi dictator before he had a chance to supply weapons of mass destruction
to the terrorists. But this was by no means the only or even—
surprising though it would seem in retrospect—the decisive consideration, either for Bush or for his supporters (or, for that matter, his opponents).

As John Podhoretz of the *New York Post* would later write:

> Those who supported the war, in overwhelming numbers, believed
> there were multiple justifications for it. Those who opposed . . . it,
> in equally overwhelming numbers, weren't swayed by the WMD
> arguments. Indeed, many of them had no difficulty opposing the
> war while believing that Saddam possessed vast quantities of such
> weapons. Take Senator Edward Kennedy: "As we have known for
> many years," he said in September 2002, "Saddam is seeking and
> developing weapons of mass destruction." And yet only a few
> weeks later he was one of twenty-three senators who voted against
> authorizing the Iraq war. Take French President Jacques Chirac,
> who believed Saddam had WMDs and still did everything in his
> power to block the war. So whether policymakers supported or op-
> posed the war effort was not determined by their conviction about
> the presence of weapons of mass destruction.

In any case, the long-range strategic rationale went beyond the
proximate causes of the invasion. Bush's idea was to extend the en-

terprise of "draining the swamps" begun in Afghanistan and then, as dictated by the first pillar of his doctrine, to set the entire region on a course toward democratization. For if Afghanistan under the Taliban represented the religious face of the terrorism bred by Islamofascist regimes, Iraq under Saddam Hussein was its most powerful secular partner. It was to deal with this two-headed beast that a two-pronged strategy was designed.

Unlike the plan to go after Afghanistan, however, the idea of invading Iraq and overthrowing Saddam Hussein provoked a firestorm scarcely less intense than the one that was still raging over Bush's insistence on using the words "good" and "evil."

Even before the debate on Iraq in particular, there had been strong objection to the whole idea of preemptive action by the United States. Some maintained that such action would be a violation of international law, while others contended that it would set a dangerous precedent under which, say, Pakistan might attack India or vice versa. But once the discussion shifted from the Bush Doctrine in general to the question of Iraq, the objections became more specific.

Most of these were brought together in early August 2002 (only about two months after Bush's speech at West Point) in a piece entitled "Don't Attack Iraq." The author was Brent Scowcroft, who had been national security adviser to the elder President Bush (and who had strongly supported the decision to leave Saddam in power after the first Gulf War of 1991). Scowcroft asserted, first, that there was

> scant evidence to tie Saddam to terrorist organizations, and even less to the September 11 attacks. Indeed Saddam's goals have little in common with the terrorists who threaten us, and there is little incentive for him to make common cause with them.

That being so, "an attack on Iraq at this time would seriously jeopardize, if not destroy, the global counterterrorist campaign we have undertaken," the campaign that must remain "our preeminent security priority."

But this was not the only "priority" that to Scowcroft was "pre-eminent":

> Possibly the most dire consequences [of attacking Saddam] would be the effect in the region. The shared view in the region is that Iraq is principally an obsession of the U.S. The obsession of the region, however, is the Israeli-Palestinian conflict.

Showing little regard for the American "obsession," Scowcroft was very solicitous of the regional one:

> If we were seen to be turning our backs on that bitter [Israeli-Palestinian] conflict . . . in order to go after Iraq, there would be an explosion of outrage against us. We would be seen as ignoring a key interest of the Muslim world in order to satisfy what is seen to be a narrow American interest.

This, added Scowcroft, "could well destabilize Arab regimes in the region," than which nothing could be worse to a quintessential realist like him.

In coming out publicly, and in these terms, against the second President Bush's policy, Scowcroft underscored the extent to which the son had diverged from the father's perspective. In addition, by lending greater credence to the already credible rumor that the elder Bush opposed invading Iraq, Scowcroft's article belied what would soon become one of the favorite theories of the hard Left—namely, that the son had gone to war in order to avenge the attempted assassination of his father.

On the other hand, by implicitly assenting to the notion that toppling Saddam was merely "a narrow American interest," Scowcroft gave a certain measure of aid and comfort to the hard Left and its fellow travelers within the liberal community. For from these circles the cry had been going out that it was the corporations, especially Halliburton (which Vice President Dick Cheney had formerly headed) and the oil companies, that were dragging us into an unnecessary war.

A similar effect flowed from Scowcroft's emphasis on resolving "the Israeli-Palestinian conflict"—a standard euphemism for putting pressure on Israel, whose "intransigence" was taken to be the major obstacle to peace. By strongly insinuating that the then Israeli prime minister, Ariel Sharon, was a greater threat to us than Saddam Hussein, Scowcroft provided a respectable rationale for the hostility toward Israel that had come shamelessly out of the closet within hours of the attacks of 9/11 and that had been growing more and more overt, more and more virulent, and more and more widespread ever since. To the "paleoconservative" Right, where the charge first surfaced in the writings of its leader, Patrick J. Buchanan, it was less the oil companies than Israel that was mainly dragging us into invading Iraq. Before long, the Left would add the same accusation to its own indictment, and in due course it would be imprinted more and more openly on large swatches of mainstream opinion.

A cognate count in this indictment held that the invasion of Iraq had been secretly engineered by a cabal of Jewish officials acting not in the interest of their own country but in the service of Israel, and more particularly of Sharon. At first the framers and early spreaders of this defamatory charge considered it the better part of prudence to identify the conspirators not as Jews but as "neoconservatives." It was a clever tactic, in that Jews did in fact constitute a large proportion of the repentant liberals and leftists who, having some twenty or thirty years earlier broken ranks with the Left and moved rightward, came to be identified as neoconservatives.* Everyone in the know knew this, and for those to whom

---

* Strictly speaking, only those who fitted this description ought to have been called neo- (i.e., new) conservatives. But partly out of ignorance and partly out of malice, the sobriquet was now applied to people like Cheney, Rumsfeld, and Rice, who had been conservatives all their lives, as well as to a number of younger hawks who had never been on the Left. It was also out of ignorance that neoconservatism was now said to have sprung from the minds of Leon Trotsky and Leo Strauss. No such notion could ever have occurred to anyone who had read or been capable of understanding the writings of Trotsky and Strauss, which were, in addition, wildly misrepresented in the diatribes against neoconservatism. Besides, the influence of these writings on the neoconservatives was (as my own case and many others demonstrated) no less wildly exaggerated.

it was news, the point could easily be gotten across by singling out only those neoconservatives who had Jewish-sounding names and ignoring the many other leading members of the group (such as Jeane Kirkpatrick, James Q. Wilson, and William J. Bennett) whose clearly non-Jewish names might confuse the picture.

This tactic had been given a trial run by Buchanan in opposing the first Gulf War of 1991. Buchanan had already been denouncing the Johnny-come-lately neoconservatives for hijacking and corrupting the conservative movement, but he now descended deeper into the fever swamps by insisting that there were "only two groups beating the drums . . . for war in the Middle East—the Israeli Defense Ministry and its amen corner in the United States." Among those standing in the "amen corner," he subsequently focused on four prominent hawks with Jewish-sounding names, counterposing them to "kids with names like McAllister, Murphy, Gonzales, and Leroy Brown" who would actually do the fighting if these Jews had their way.

Ten years later, in 2001, in Buchanan's articles, as well as in those produced by other paleoconservatives within the journalistic fraternity (including Robert Novak, Arnaud de Borchgrave, and Paul Craig Roberts), one of the four hawks of 1991, Richard Perle, made a return appearance. But Perle was now joined in starring roles by Paul Wolfowitz and Douglas Feith, both of whom occupied high positions in the Pentagon, and a large supporting cast of identifiably Jewish intellectuals and commentators outside the government (among them Charles Krauthammer, William Kristol, and Robert Kagan). Like their predecessors in 1991, the members of the new ensemble were portrayed as agents of their bellicose counterparts in the Israeli government. But there was also a difference: the new group had allegedly managed to infiltrate the upper reaches of the American government. Having pulled this off, they had conspired to manipulate their non-Jewish bosses—Vice President Dick Cheney, Secretary of Defense Donald Rumsfeld, National Security Adviser Condoleezza Rice, and George W. Bush himself—into invading Iraq.

Before long, this theory was picked up and circulated by just about everyone in the whole world who was intent on discrediting the Bush Doctrine. And understandably so, for what could suit their purposes better than to "expose" the invasion of Iraq—and by extension the whole of World War IV—as a war started by Jews and being waged solely in the interest of Israel? Nor were they deterred or given pause by the simple fact that the great majority of American Jews, while supporting Israel, *opposed* the invasion of Iraq, or that the Israelis themselves were more worried about Iran than about Iraq. Thus, Buchanan, in what was probably the most brazen version of the theory, could write:

> *Cui bono?* For whose benefit these endless wars in a region that holds nothing vital to America save oil, which the Arabs must sell us to survive? Who would benefit from a war of civilizations between the West and Islam? Answer: one nation, one leader, one party. Israel, Sharon, Likud.*

Still, most other purveyors of this theory continued to pretend that when they said "neocon"—the abbreviated version that soon became common—they did not mean "Jew." Yet the theory inescapably rested on all-too-familiar anti-Semitic canards—principally that Jews were never reliably loyal to the country in which they lived and that they were always conspiring behind the scenes, often successfully, to manipulate the world for their own nefarious purposes. The classic expression of this fantasy was, of course, *The Protocols of the Elders of Zion*, a document that had been forged by the Czarist secret police in the late nineteenth century and had more recently been resurrected and distributed by the millions throughout the Arab-Muslim world (even serving as the basis of an immensely popular, ten-part television series produced in Egypt). But far from remaining confined to the Arab-Muslim world, the themes of the *Protocols* were surfacing throughout the

---

* Note the echo here of Hitler's *Ein Volk, Ein Reich, Ein Fuhrer* ("One People, One Empire, One Leader"), which slyly identifies Israel with Nazi Germany.

West as well, and the main agency of transmission was the non-stop and universal carry-on over the "neocons." The hands of the Bush Doctrine may, in this view, have been the hands of George Bush, but the voice was the voice of the neocon ventriloquists who were using him as their dummy.

Quite apart from its pernicious moral and political implications, the charge had been risible in connection with the first George Bush, whose hostility to Israel was not that much less intense than Buchanan's. But even in connection with the strongly pro-Israel second George Bush, it was equally ridiculous. To begin with, it asked one to believe the unbelievable: that strong-minded people like Bush, Rumsfeld, Cheney, and Rice could be fooled by a bunch of cunning subordinates, whether Jewish or not, into doing anything at all against their better judgment, let alone something so momentous as waging a war, let alone a war in which they could detect no clear relation to American interests.

In the second place, there was the evidence uncovered by the purveyors of this theory themselves. That evidence, to which they triumphantly pointed, consisted of published articles and statements in which the alleged conspirators had for years been openly and unambiguously advocating the very policies that they now stood accused of having secretly foisted upon an unwary Bush administration. In any case, it was not until 9/11 that these ideas were embraced by Bush. And the reason he did so then was that they offered the most cogent and coherent articulation available of what he himself intuitively felt and understood—both about Al Qaeda and about Saddam Hussein.*

So far as that went, the supposedly secret conspirators had never concealed their belief that toppling Saddam Hussein and adopting a policy aimed at the democratization of the entire Middle East would be good not only for the United States and for the people of the region but also for Israel. (And what, an unchar-

---

* It was in much the same sense that, after the Soviet invasion of Afghanistan and the seizure of the American hostages in Iran in 1979, Ronald Reagan had been influenced by an earlier generation of neoconservatives.

acteristically puzzled Richard Perle asked a hostile interviewer, was wrong with that?) Which brings us to the fourth and final pillar on which the Bush Doctrine was erected.

Listening to the laments of Brent Scowcroft and many others, one would think that George W. Bush had been ignoring "the Israeli-Palestinian conflict" altogether in his misplaced "obsession" with Iraq. In fact, however, even before 9/11 it had been widely and authoritatively reported that Bush was planning to come out publicly in favor of establishing a Palestinian state as the only path to a peaceful resolution of the conflict, and in October, after a short delay caused by 9/11, he became the first American president actually to do so. Yet at some point in the evolution of his thinking over the months that followed, Bush seems to have realized that there was something bizarre about supporting the establishment of a Palestinian state that would be run by a terrorist like the then president of the Palestinian Authority, Yasir Arafat, and his henchmen. Why should the United States acquiesce, let alone help, in adding yet another state to those harboring and sponsoring terrorism precisely at a time when we were at war to rid the world of just such regimes?

Presumably it was under the prodding of this question that, about nine months after he had first promulgated his new doctrine, Bush came up with an idea even more novel in its way than the new conception of terrorism he had developed in response to 9/11. Thus, on June 24, 2002, he issued a statement adding conditions to his endorsement of a Palestinian state:

> Today, Palestinian authorities are encouraging, not opposing terrorism. This is unacceptable. And the United States will not support the establishment of a Palestinian state until its leaders engage in a sustained fight against the terrorists and dismantle their infrastructure.

But engaging in such a fight, he added, required the election of "new leaders, leaders not compromised by terror," who would embark on building "entirely new political and economic institutions based on democracy, market economics, and action against terrorism."

It was with these words that Bush brought his "vision" (as he kept calling it) of a Palestinian state living peacefully alongside Israel into line with his overall perspective on the evil of terrorism. And having traveled that far, he went the distance by repositioning the Palestinian issue in the larger context from which Arab propaganda had ripped it. Strangely enough, this move attracted as little attention as the preemption pillar had before it, and yet it represented nothing less than a repudiation of the conventional wisdom about the Palestinian issue. Let me try to explain why and how it did so.

Even before Israel was born in 1948, the Muslim countries of the Middle East had been fighting against the establishment of a sovereign Jewish state—any Jewish state—on land they believed Allah had reserved for those faithful to his prophet Muhammad. Hence, the Arab-Israeli conflict had pitted hundreds of millions of Arabs and other Muslims, in control of more than two dozen countries and vast stretches of territory, not to mention a stranglehold on global oil supplies, against a handful of Jews who then numbered well under three-quarters of a million and who lived on a sliver of land so tiny that it could comfortably have fit into New Jersey. But then came the Six-Day War of 1967. Launched by the then Egyptian president, Gamal Abdel Nasser, in an openly declared effort to wipe Israel off the map and push its Jewish inhabitants into the sea, it ended instead with Israel in control of the West Bank (formerly occupied by Jordan) and Gaza (which had been controlled by Egypt). This humiliating defeat, however, was eventually turned into a great victory by Arab propagandists who redefined the ongoing war of the whole Muslim world against the Jewish state as, instead, a struggle merely between the Palestinians and the Israelis. Thus was Israel's image transformed from a David into a Goliath, a move that succeeded in alienating much of the old sympathy—especially on the Left—that had previously been enjoyed by the outnumbered and besieged Jewish state.

Bush now reversed this reversal. Not only did he reconstruct a truthful framework by telling the Palestinian people that they had been treated for decades "as pawns in the Middle East conflict." He also insisted on being open and forthright about the nations that belonged in this larger picture and about what they had been up to:

> I've said in the past that nations are either with us or against us in the war on terror. To be counted on the side of peace, nations must act. Every leader actually committed to peace will end incitement to violence in official media and publicly denounce homicide bombs. Every nation actually committed to peace will stop the flow of money, equipment, and recruits to terrorist groups seeking the destruction of Israel, including Hamas, Islamic Jihad, and Hezbollah. Every nation committed to peace must block the shipment of Iranian supplies to these groups and oppose regimes that promote terror, like Iraq. And Syria must choose the right side in the war on terror by closing terrorist camps and expelling terrorist organizations.

Here, then, Bush restored the context in which to understand the narrower Middle East conflict. In the months ahead, pressured by his main European ally, the British prime minister Tony Blair, and by his own secretary of State, Colin Powell, Bush would sometimes seem to backslide into the old way of thinking. But he would invariably recover. Nor would he ever lose sight of the "vision" by which he was guided on this issue and through which he had simultaneously made a strong start in fitting not the Palestinian Authority alone but the entire Muslim world, "friends" no less than enemies, into his conception of the war against terrorism.

With the inconsistency thus removed and the resultant shakiness repaired by the addition of this fourth pillar to undergird it, the Bush Doctrine was now firm, coherent, and complete.

CHAPTER FOUR

FROM WORLD WAR III
TO WORLD WAR IV

B OTH AS A theoretical construct and as a guide to policy, the new Bush Doctrine could not have been further from the "Vietnam syndrome"—the loss of self-confidence and the concomitant spread of neo-isolationist and pacifist sentiment throughout the American body politic, and most prominently into the elite institutions of American culture, that began during the last years of the Vietnam War. I have already pointed to a likeness between the Truman Doctrine's declaration that World War III had started and the Bush Doctrine's equally portentous declaration that 9/11 had plunged us into World War IV. But fully to measure the distance traveled by the Bush Doctrine, I want to look now at the other presidential doctrines that preceded it, beginning with the one developed by Richard Nixon in the late 1960s precisely in response to the Vietnam syndrome.

Contrary to legend, our military intervention in Vietnam under John F. Kennedy in the early 1960s, far from being unpopular, was backed by every sector of mainstream opinion as a legitimate application of containment. In such bastions of the old foreign policy establishment as the Council on Foreign Relations and the Brookings Institution, and in periodicals like the *New York Times*, the *Washington Post, Time*, and *Newsweek*, the consensus was that saving South Vietnam from a Communist takeover was a vital interest of the United States. The prevailing attitude was perfectly expressed in a *Times* editorial under the headline "Prospects in Vietnam." It began by speaking of "Communist aggression" against South Vietnam that had been "launched as a calculated and deliberate operation by the Communist leaders of the North" and ended with the admonition that "Free World forces . . . still have a chance in South Vietnam, and every effort should be made to save the situation." Even as late as 1965, when the originally minuscule antiwar movement was beginning to pick up steam, David Halberstam, who had been the *Times* correspondent in Vietnam in the early days and would subsequently write in derisive and contemptuous terms about the American involvement there, still believed that

> Vietnam is a legitimate part of the [U.S.] global commitment . . . perhaps one of only five or six nations of the world that is truly vital to U.S. interests.

At least up until 1965, indeed, virtually the only criticism from the mainstream concerned such tactical issues as how best to fight the new kind of war Vietnam represented. But with Lyndon B. Johnson having succeeded Kennedy in the White House, doubts began to arise about the political wisdom of the intervention: was it perhaps "the wrong war, in the wrong place, at the wrong time"—an unwise extension of containment to a situation for which it had not been designed and to a region in which it did not apply? What, however, would turn out to be more decisive than doubts like these were the questions that were being asked within ever-widening circles of the intellectual community. These questions were not about whether the war was being conducted effectively or whether it really did represent a proper application of containment; they were about whether we had any right to fight it at all.

No sooner asked than answered: to the writers and academics and the student radicals who were raising these questions, what the United States was doing in Vietnam was immoral at best, and positively evil at worst. With few exceptions, even those in the antiwar camp who dissociated themselves from the view that the Communists deserved to win and that "Amerika"—as the radicals took to spelling the name in order to suggest an association with Nazi Germany—was waging a criminal war did so not because they were outraged by this kind of talk but because it "gave the movement a bad name" and made it difficult to recruit "ordinary people" into its ranks.

Nevertheless, by the time Richard Nixon had replaced Johnson in 1968, a surprisingly large number of "ordinary people"—even if not large enough to prevail at the polls—had successfully been recruited. Even more surprisingly, most of the not-so-ordinary people who had led the country into Vietnam were now scurrying to join the antiwar parade and even to get to the head of it. Most of them justified this turnabout by claiming that, thanks to Johnson's blunders, the war could no longer be won, but there were others who, while still pretending that Kennedy's decision to intervene had not been a folly, went all the way with the radicals in proclaiming that under Johnson it had grown into a crime.

To this new political reality the Nixon Doctrine was a reluctant accommodation. As going into Vietnam under the aegis of containment had worked to undermine support for that strategy, Nixon—along with his chief adviser in foreign affairs, Henry Kissinger—thought that getting out of Vietnam could, if managed in the right way, conversely work to create the new strategy that had become necessary.

First, American forces would be withdrawn gradually, while the South Vietnamese built up enough power to assume responsibility for the defense of their own country. The American role would then be limited to providing arms and equipment. The same policy, suitably modified according to local circumstances, would be applied to the rest of the world as well. In every major region, the United States would now depend on local surrogates rather than on its own military to deter or contain any Soviet-

sponsored aggression, or any other potentially destabilizing occur-
rence. We would supply arms and other forms of assistance, but
henceforth the deterring and the fighting would be left to others.
Thus did the Truman Doctrine give way to the Nixon Doctrine,
and containment to strategic retreat.

To be sure, the new policy did not call itself by any such unat-
tractive name as "strategic retreat." It was called "détente," and in
the eyes of Nixon and Kissinger, it did not—as critics like me
charged at the time—amount to a wholesale repudiation of the
Truman Doctrine and even a surrender to appeasement. To its authors, it represented, rather, the highest degree of containment
compatible with the post-Vietnam political climate—a climate in
which Congress, supported by the leading centers of opinion
within the foreign policy establishment, the major news media,
and the intellectual community, wanted only to curtail American
commitments abroad to a sparse minimum and to cut back dras-
tically on defense spending.

But whereas Nixon and Kissinger saw détente as an adaptation
of containment to a set of changing circumstances—the best, in
effect, one could now hope to do—Jimmy Carter, who became
president in 1976 after the short interregnum of Gerald Ford,
seemed to see no need for containment at all. Whether in the
Trumanesque form of American military power or in the Nixonian
modification of local surrogates supported by American arms, containment in Carter's view had become obsolete. He made this as
plain as plain could be in one of his first major speeches on foreign
policy. There he declared that "historical trends [had] weakened
the foundation" of the two principles that had guided our foreign
policy in the past:

> a belief that Soviet expansionism was almost inevitable and that
> it must be contained. . . . Being confident of our own future, we
> are now free of that inordinate fear of Communism which once
> led us to embrace any dictator who joined us in that fear. I'm glad
> that's being changed.

One of the prime examples of such dictators was the Shah of Iran, who, under the Nixon Doctrine, had been designated a "pillar" of American security in the Persian Gulf, but whose hold on power was now being threatened by an uprising of Muslim fundamentalists led by the violently anti-American Ayatollah Khomeini. If the Nixon Doctrine had remained in force, it would have called upon us to support the Shah in doing whatever was necessary to stave off a revolution that might or might not have been good for the Soviet Union but was certainly bad for the United States. Whether Richard Nixon himself would have had the stomach and the political base for such a policy—involving, as it would have done, American acquiescence in the massacre by Iranian troops of many thousands of demonstrators—is open to serious doubt. In any event, Richard Nixon was gone, and the doctrine bearing his name was not about to be disinterred by a president who saw no need for it and even thought that the United States would be better off without allies like the Shah. And so—in what would seem in retrospect an unrecognized harbinger of World War IV—the Shah was toppled by the Ayatollah Khomeini. Just how blind the Carter administration was to this portentous development can be gauged by the fact that Andrew Young, Carter's own ambassador to the UN, hailed the radical Islamist despot now ruling Iran as a saint and a great believer in human rights.

We have already seen how the seizure of American hostages by Iranian "students," followed by the Soviet invasion of Afghanistan, exposed the twin delusions of Carter's foreign policy—even, it appeared, to Carter himself. Hence, "mature restraint" was shelved, and a new Carter Doctrine took its place. In effect recanting his former repudiation of containment and presenting himself as a born-again Truman Democrat, Carter now declared that

> an attempt by any outside force to gain control of the Persian
> Gulf region will be regarded as an assault on the vital interests of

the U.S. . . . . [and] will be repelled by use of any means necessary, including military force.

But this conversion to containment came too late to erase the bitter taste left by Carter's weak response to Iran and Afghanistan. It therefore failed to fend off the challenge of Ronald Reagan, who soundly trounced him in the presidential election of 1980.

Because Reagan's rhetoric was so tough, and because he put his money where his mouth was in pushing through a big increase in defense spending, the impression was created that he too had repudiated containment, only from the other side. Both his warmest friends and his bitterest enemies even imagined that he was resurrecting the old idea of "liberation" or "rollback" that had been advocated by the right wing of the Republican Party back in the 1950s, when it was denouncing containment as a cowardly strategy. This impression was reinforced by the doctrine that Reagan in his turn promulgated at the start of his second term.

The Reagan Doctrine was intended as a counter to the Brezhnev Doctrine through which the then Soviet leader had declared that (as Reagan's secretary of state, George Shultz, summarized it) "what's mine is mine, what's yours is up for grabs." Rejecting this meant that the United States would come to the aid of any government (such as the one in El Salvador) or any insurgency (such as the one in Nicaragua) that was resisting a Communist takeover.

Yet it was only by contrast with Carter's "mature restraint" that this looked like "rollback" or "liberation." What it actually added up to was a return to containment—not (as I myself mistakenly argued at the time) in the milder Nixonian form of "détente," but in the robust version outlined by Truman. Indeed, even Reagan's language echoed the speech in which the Truman Doctrine had been announced. Truman:

It must be the policy of the United States to support free peoples who are resisting attempted subjugation by armed minorities or by outside pressure.

Now Reagan:

> We must not break faith with those who are risking their
> lives . . . on every continent, from Afghanistan to Nicaragua . . .
> to defy Soviet aggression and secure rights which have been ours
> from birth. Support for freedom fighters is self-defense.

It was by returning to this policy and building on it that Reagan
set the stage for its ultimate vindication in the fall of the Soviet
empire.

In the twelve years that elapsed between the completion of
Reagan's two terms and the beginning of George W. Bush's first
term came the administrations of George H. W. Bush and Bill
Clinton, neither of whom left a doctrine behind. The elder Bush's
most dramatic act in the field of foreign policy was the successful
ousting of Saddam Hussein from Kuwait in the first Gulf War of
1991. But—to repeat a point I made earlier—in settling for a
restoration of the status quo ante instead of going on to topple the
Iraqi despot, the elder Bush was true to his beliefs as a "realist"
that his job (except with respect to Israel) was to maintain stability, or, when stability was upset, to restore it, and that the internal character of a regime was nobody's business but its own. Yet
as 9/11 would make clear to the next President Bush, this policy
took no account whatsoever of the Islamist terrorism that was already showing itself to be a new cause of instability in the Middle
East as well as a threat to the United States. And by failing to recognize that Saddam was lending support to various terrorist
groups, the elder Bush demonstrated a blindness to the crucial role
of state sponsorship in this growing threat that was hardly less
complete than Carter's with respect to the Ayatollah Khomeini.

As for Clinton, his passions (again, except with respect to
Israel) were most fully engaged by domestic, not foreign, affairs,
and even though he surprisingly turned out to be less averse to the
use of force than his past hostility to everything military had led
one to expect, his interventions (as in Bosnia and Kosovo) were
hesitant, uncertain, and driven by strictly humanitarian consider-

ations. (I once quipped that he used military force only when no American interest was at stake.) Neither a realist like the elder Bush nor a "hard" Wilsonian like Reagan, Clinton could afford to concentrate most of his attention on domestic concerns because his two terms in office were "years of relative quiet, years of repose, years of sabbatical."

These words were spoken by George W. Bush in his Second Inaugural Address, and they were immediately followed by the shock of "—and then there came a day of fire." Actually, as we have seen, this fire had first broken out long before 9/11 and had been burning with ever greater intensity during the Clinton "years of sabbatical" and through the first eight months of George Bush's presidency. But it was only with 9/11 that its larger significance as the start of another world war became blazingly clear to Bush. Out of that recognition his new doctrine was born, and while it bore an analogical or situational resemblance to the Truman Doctrine in that it too was designed to confront a new totalitarian menace, it departed from containment to a much greater extent than Reagan had seemed to do or than Nixon had actually done.

Thus, instead of the withdrawal and fallback that constituted the essence of the Nixon Doctrine, Bush proposed a highly ambitious forward strategy of intervention. Instead of relying on local surrogates, Bush proposed an active deployment of our own military power. Instead of deterrence, Bush proposed preemption and "taking the fight to the enemy." Instead of worrying about the stability of the region in question, Bush proposed to destabilize it through "regime change." And instead of the feeling that the United States had suffered a failure of nerve and no longer had the will to pursue a serious strategy of standing up to the Soviet Union, Bush believed that this country had rediscovered its mission in the world and possessed the courage to pursue it.

On this last point, Bush was following in the optimistic footsteps of Ronald Reagan, who had lifted the country out of the Carter "malaise" with his celebrations of America as "a city upon a hill," his supreme confidence that we would eventually triumph over the evil empire, and his conviction that "the future belongs to the free." But there was also a big difference here. Reagan's arms buildup, together with his refusal to accept the Brezhnev Doctrine of "what's mine is mine, and what's yours is up for grabs," signified a return to containment and deterrence. Bush, however, believed that this very strategy had been rendered obsolete by 9/11. To cite the relevant passage again:

> For much of the last century, America's defense relied on the cold war doctrines of deterrence and containment. In some cases, those strategies still apply. But new threats also require new thinking. Deterrence—the promise of massive retaliation against nations— means nothing against shadowy terrorist networks with no nation or citizens to defend. . . . Containment is not possible when unbalanced dictators with weapons of mass destruction can deliver those weapons or missiles or secretly provide them to terrorist allies.

The Nixon Doctrine had obviously emerged out of the post-Vietnam climate of opinion, just as Reagan's foreign policy had harmonized with the resurgent popular will revealed by his own election to reverse the decline of American power. What about the Bush Doctrine? Was the political and military strategy it put forward comparably in tune with the post-9/11 public mood?

CHAPTER FIVE

"JACKAL BINS"
THEN AND NOW

ERTAINLY IN THE immediate aftermath of 9/11 the Bush
Doctrine seemed to be in perfect harmony with the prevailing mood in the country. Looking around them, several younger commentators, like James Taranto of the *Wall Street
Journal* and David Brooks, then of the *Weekly Standard* and later a
New York Times columnist, were even quick to proclaim the birth
of an entirely new era in American history. What December 7,
1941, had done to the old isolationism, they announced,
September 11, 2001, had done to the Vietnam syndrome. It was
politically dead, and the cultural fallout of that war—all the damaging changes wrought by the 1960s and the 1970s—would now
follow it into the grave.

The most obvious sign of the new era was that once again we
were saluting our now ubiquitously displayed flag. This was the
very flag that, not so long ago, leftist radicals had thought fit only
for burning. Yet now, even on the old flag-burning Left, a few
prominent personalities were painfully wrenching their unaccus-
tomed arms into something vaguely resembling a salute.

It was a scene reminiscent of the response of some Communists
to the suppression by the new Soviet regime of the sailors' revolt
that erupted in Kronstadt in the early 1920s. Far more murderous
horrors would pour out of the malignant recesses of Stalinist rule,

but as the first in that long series of atrocities leading to disillusionment with the Soviet Union, Kronstadt became the portent of them all. In its own way, 9/11 became—if, as it would turn out, only temporarily—an inverse Kronstadt for a number of radical leftists of the early twenty-first century. What it did was raise questions about what one of them (Todd Gitlin, a leading figure in the New Left of the sixties and now a professor at Columbia) was honest enough to describe as their inveterately "negative faith in America the ugly."

September 11 also brought to mind a poem by the transplanted English poet W. H. Auden written upon the outbreak of World War II and entitled "September 1, 1939." Although it contained hostile sentiments about America—atavistic remnants of Auden's own Communist period as a young man in England—the opening lines seemed so evocative of September 11, 2001, that they were often quoted in the early days of this new war:

> *I sit in one of the dives*
> *On Fifty-second Street*
> *Uncertain and afraid*
> *As the clever hopes expire*
> *Of a low dishonest decade.*

Auden's low dishonest decade was the 1930s, with its clever hopes centered on the construction of a workers' paradise in the Soviet Union. Our counterpart was the 1960s and its less clever hopes centered not on construction, however illusory, but on destruction—the destruction of the institutions that made up the American way of life. For America was conceived in that period as the great obstacle to any improvement in the lot of the wretched of the earth, not least those within its own borders.

Having broken ranks with the Left precisely because I was repelled by its "negative faith in America the ugly," I naturally welcomed this new patriotic mood with open arms. It seemed to me a sign of greater intellectual sanity and moral health, and I fervently hoped that it would last. But I could not fully share the heady confidence of some of my younger political friends that the change was permanent—that, as they exulted, nothing in American politics and American culture would ever be the same again. As a veteran of the political and cultural wars of the 1960s, I knew from my own scars how ephemeral such a mood might well turn out to be, and how vulnerable it was to seemingly insignificant forces.

In this connection, I was haunted by one memory in particular. It was of an evening in the year 1960, when I went to address a meeting of left-wing radicals on a subject that had then barely begun to show the whites of its eyes: the possibility of American military involvement in a faraway place called Vietnam. Accompanying me that evening was the late Marion Magid, a member of my staff at *Commentary*, of which I had recently become the editor. As we entered the drafty old hall on Union Square in Manhattan, Marion surveyed the fifty or so people in the audience and whispered to me: "Do you realize that every young person in this room is a tragedy to some family or other?"

The memory of this quip brought back to life some sense of how unpromising the future had then appeared to be for that bedraggled-looking assemblage. No one would have dreamed that these young people, and the generation about to descend from them politically and culturally, would within the blink of a historical eye come to be hailed as "the best informed, the most intelligent, and the most idealistic this country has ever known." Those words, even more incredibly, would emanate from what the new movement regarded as the very belly of the beast: from, to be specific, Archibald Cox, a professor at the Harvard Law School and later solicitor general of the United States. Similar encomia would flow unctuously from the mouths of parents, teachers, clergymen, artists, and journalists.

More incredible yet, the ideas and attitudes of the new movement, cleaned up but essentially unchanged, would within a mere ten years turn one of our two major parties upside down and inside out. By 1972, only eleven years after President John F. Kennedy had promised that we would "pay any price, bear any burden . . . to assure the survival and the success of liberty," George McGovern, nominated for president by Kennedy's own party, was campaigning on the antiwar slogan "Come Home, America." It was a slogan that to an uncanny degree reflected the ethos of the embryonic movement I had addressed in Union Square only about a decade before.

In going over this familiar ground, I am trying to make two points. One is that the nascent radical movement of the late 1950s and early 1960s was up against an adversary, namely, the "Establishment," that looked unassailable. Even so—and this is my second point—to the bewilderment of almost everyone, not least the radicals themselves, they blew and they blew and they blew the house down.

Here we had a major development that slipped in under the radar of virtually all the pundits and the trend-spotters. How well I remember John Roche, a political scientist then working in the Johnson White House, being quoted by the columnist Jimmy Breslin as having derisively labeled the radicals a bunch of "Upper West Side jackal bins." As further investigation disclosed, Roche had actually said "Jacobins," a word so unfamiliar to his interviewer that in transcribing his notes, "jackal bins" was the best Breslin could do.

Much ink has been spilled, gallons of it by me, in the struggle to explain how and why a great "Establishment" representing so wide a national consensus could have been toppled so easily and so quickly by so small and marginal a group as these "jackal bins." In the domain of foreign affairs, of course, the usual answer is Vietnam. In this view, it was by deciding to fight an unpopular war that the Establishment rendered itself vulnerable.

The ostensible problem with this explanation is—to say once more what, judging from the pertinacity of the myth, cannot be said too often—that at least until 1965 Vietnam was a popular war. In fact, even when all but one or two of the people who either had directly led us into Vietnam or had applauded our intervention commenced falling all over themselves in a race to join the antiwar parade, public opinion continued supporting the war.

Here I can offer the evidence of another memory—this one of a meeting with Lyndon B. Johnson in the Oval Office in 1965. One of his assistants, Richard Goodwin, who would himself later rush to join the antiwar parade, had brought me there for the express purpose of warning the president that the tide was turning against the war. But before I could even get the words out of my mouth, Johnson pulled a bunch of public opinion polls out of his pocket and read me the numbers that supposedly made nonsense of what I was trying to say. Very likely he had already been told by John Roche that his only opponents were those "jackal bins" on the Upper West Side of Manhattan and that they were so small and politically powerless a gang that he had nothing to worry about from them.

But Roche could not have been more mistaken. As Johnson would discover in the next few years, the polls on which he was leaning were the weakest of weak reeds. For in an almost unbelievable and probably unprecedented development, public opinion had ceased to count. Indeed, as the Tet offensive launched by the Communists in 1968 revealed, reality itself had ceased to count. All serious students of the war would later come to agree with what some had vainly struggled to say at the time—namely, that Tet had been a crushing defeat not for us but for the North Vietnamese and the Vietcong. Don Oberdorfer of the *Washington Post* would sum it all up in his authoritative book on the subject:

> It is clear that the attack forces—and particularly the indigenous Vietcong, who did most of the fighting and dying—suffered a grievous military setback. Tens of thousands of the most dedicated and experienced fighters emerged from the jungles and forests of the countryside only to meet a deadly rain of fire and steel within the cities. The Vietcong lost the best of a generation of resistance fighters, and . . . because the people of the cities did

not rise up against the foreigners and puppets at Tet . . . the Communist claim to a moral and political authority in South Vietnam suffered a serious blow.

Nevertheless, the almost universal impression created by press and television coverage of the offensive was of a great defeat for the Americans and the South Vietnamese. On every point the situation was misrepresented by misleading stories and pictures and in some cases by outright falsehood. All of which set the stage for the entrance of Walter Cronkite, who, as the avuncular anchor of the *CBS Evening News*, was the "most trusted man in America." Cronkite had only to set his imprimatur on the illusion that Tet had been a defeat for us, and a defeat it became.

Admittedly, in *electoral* politics, where numbers are decisive, public opinion remained potent. Consequently, none of the doves contending for the Democratic presidential nomination in 1968 could beat Johnson's vice president Hubert Humphrey—not Eugene McCarthy and not, in all likelihood, Robert F. Kennedy if he had lived to finish the race. Yet Humphrey was forced to take several giant steps away from his erstwhile support of the war, and even his Republican opponent, Richard Nixon, a notoriously hawkish anti-Communist, felt it necessary to campaign on the claim that he had a "plan" not for winning but for getting us out of Vietnam (with, to be sure, our honor intact). Four years later, in 1972, with his plan still not executed, Nixon nonetheless won by a landslide against George McGovern, a more authentic dove than either McCarthy or Kennedy. But this victory was widely attributed to the famous announcement by Henry Kissinger that "peace is at hand."*

All of which is to say that, on Vietnam, elite opinion trumped popular opinion. Nor were the effects restricted to foreign policy.

---

* Both Nixon and Kissinger emphatically, and plausibly, denied that this announcement had been an election-eve ploy. Yet even if they did not intend it as such, there seems little question that it brought more than a merely marginal benefit.

They extended into the newly antagonistic attitude toward everything America was and represented.

It hardly needs stressing that this attitude found a home in the world of the arts, the universities, and the major media of news and entertainment, where intellectuals shaped by the 1960s and their acolytes in the publishing houses of New York and in the studios of Hollywood held sway. But it would be a serious mistake to suppose that the trickle-down effect of the professoriate's attitude was confined to literature, journalism, and show business.

John Maynard Keynes once said that "practical men who believe themselves to be quite exempt from any intellectual influences, are usually the slaves of some defunct economist." Keynes was referring specifically to businessmen. But practical functionaries like bureaucrats and administrators were subject to the same rule, though they tended to be the slaves not of economists but of historians and sociologists and philosophers and novelists who were very much alive even when their ideas had, or should have, become defunct. Nor was it necessary for the "practical men" to have studied the works in question, or even ever to have heard of their authors. All they needed to do was read the *New York Times*, or switch on their television sets, or go to the movies—and, drip by drip, a more easily assimilable form of the original material was absorbed into their heads and their nervous systems. By this process could a minority win out over a majority—or to put it another way, could culture trump politics.

It was because I had seen how this process worked that I had my doubts as to whether the terrorist attacks of September 11, 2001, would turn out to mark a genuine turning point comparable to the bombing of Pearl Harbor on December 7, 1941. Before Pearl Harbor, several groups ranging across the political spectrum had fought against our joining the British, who had been at war with Nazi Germany since 1939. There were the isolationists, both liberal and conservative, who detected no American interest in so distant a conflict; there were the right-wing radicals who thought that if we were going to go to war, it ought to be on the side of

Nazi Germany against Communist Russia, not the other way around; and there were the left-wing radicals who saw the war as a struggle between two equally malign imperialistic systems in which they had no stake. Under the influence of these groups, a decisive majority of Americans had opposed our entry into the war right up to the moment of the Japanese attack on Pearl Harbor. But from that moment on, the opposition faded away. The anti-war groups either lost most of their members or lapsed into a morose silence, and public opinion did a 180-degree turn.

At first, September 11 did seem to resemble Pearl Harbor in its galvanizing effect, while by all indications the first big American offensive of World War IV—the campaign in Afghanistan—was supported by a perhaps even larger percentage of the public than Vietnam had been at the beginning. Nevertheless, even though the opposition in 2001 was still numerically insignificant, it was much stronger than it had been in the early days of Vietnam. The reason was that it now maintained a tight grip over the institutions that, in the later stages of the Vietnam War, had been surrendered bit by bit to the anti-American Left.

There was, for openers, the literary community, which could stand in for the world of the arts in general. No sooner had the twin towers been toppled and the Pentagon smashed than a fierce competition began for the gold in the anti-American Olympics. Susan Sontag seized an early lead in this contest with a piece in which she asserted that 9/11 was an attack "undertaken as a consequence of specific American alliances and actions." Not content with suggesting that we had brought this aggression on ourselves, she went on to compare the backing in Congress for our "robotic President" to "the unanimously applauded, self-congratulatory bromides of a Soviet Party Congress."

Norman Mailer, surprisingly slow out of the starting gate, soon came up strong on the inside by comparing the twin towers to "two huge buck teeth" and pronouncing the ruins at Ground Zero "more beautiful than the buildings were." Still playing the enfant terrible even as he was closing in on his eightieth birthday, Mailer denounced us as "cultural oppressors and aesthetic oppressors" of the Third World. In what did this oppression consist? It consisted, he expatiated, in our establishing "enclaves of our food out there, like McDonald's," and in putting "our high-rise buildings" around the airports of even "the meanest, scummiest, capital[s] in the world." For these horrendous crimes we had, on 9/11, received a measure—and only a small measure at that—of our just deserts.

Then there were the universities. A report issued shortly after 9/11 by the American Council of Trustees and Alumni (ACTA) cited about one hundred malodorous statements wafting out of campuses all over the country that resembled Sontag and Mailer in blaming the attacks not on the terrorists but on America. Among these were three especially choice specimens. From a professor at the University of New Mexico: "Anyone who can blow up the Pentagon gets my vote." From a professor at Rutgers: "[We] should be aware that the ultimate cause [of 9/11] is the fascism of U.S. foreign policy over the past many decades." And from a professor at the University of Massachusetts: "[The American flag] is a symbol of terrorism and death and fear and destruction and oppression."

When the ACTA report was issued, protesting wails of "McCarthyism" were heard throughout the land, especially from the professors cited. Like them, Susan Sontag, too, claimed that her freedom of speech was being placed in jeopardy. In this peculiar reading of the First Amendment, much favored by leftists in general, they were free to say anything they liked, but the right to free speech ended where criticism of what they had said began.

In fact, with rare exceptions, most attempts to stifle dissent on the campus were directed at the many students and the few faculty members who supported the 9/11 war. All these attempts could be encapsulated into a single phenomenon: on a number of campuses, students or professors who displayed American flags or patriotic posters were forced to take them down. As for Susan Sontag's freedom of speech, hardly had the ink dried on her post-9/11 piece than she became the subject of countless fawning reports and interviews in periodicals and on television programs around the world.

Speaking of television, it was soon drowning us with material presenting Islam in glowing terms. Mainly, these programs took their cue from the president and other political leaders, who were then still striving so mightily to deny that the war against terrorism was a war against Islam that they could not bring themselves to name the enemy who had declared war on us and against whom we were fighting.

But it was from the universities, not from the politicians, that the substantive content of these broadcasts derived, in interviews with academics, many of them Muslims themselves, whose accounts of Islam were selectively roseate. Sometimes they were even downright untruthful, especially in sanitizing the doctrine of jihad. (They claimed it meant only the individual's internal struggle for holiness and not holy war against apostates and infidels.) They also minimized the extent to which leading Muslim clerics all over the world had been celebrating suicide bombers as heroes and martyrs—not excluding those who had crashed into the World Trade Center and the Pentagon.

Here we had another case study in the continued workings of the trickle-down effect I have already described. Thus, hard on the heels of 9/11, the universities began adding innumerable courses on Islam to their curricula. On the campus, "understanding Islam" inevitably translated into apologetics for the grievances of the Muslim world against us, and most of the media dutifully followed suit. The media also adopted the stance of neutrality between the terrorists and ourselves that prevailed among the relatively moderate professoriate, as when the major television networks ordered their anchors to avoid exhibiting partisanship.

The great exception was the Fox News Channel. In an article deploring the fact that Fox was covering the war from a frankly pro-American perspective, the *New York Times* expressed relief that no other network had so cavalierly discarded the sacred conventions dictating that journalists, in the words of David Westin, the president of ABC News, must "maintain their neutrality in times of war." Of course, "neutrality" between America and its Islamofascist enemies logically implied that the two were morally equivalent, which was bad enough. But, worse yet, instead of providing objectivity, "neutrality" in practice would (as will become evident later on) produce an antiwar and in many cases anti-American stance as an alternative to the pro-American Fox. And instead of being frank about this, the networks would vehemently deny that they were saying what they were saying and doing what they were doing.

Although the vast majority of those who blamed America for having been attacked were on the Left, a few voices on the Right joined this perverted chorus. Speaking on Pat Robertson's TV program, the Reverend Jerry Falwell delivered himself of the view that God was punishing the United States for the moral decay exemplified by a variety of liberal groups among us. Both later apologized for singling out these groups, but each continued to insist that God was withdrawing His protection from America because all of us had become great sinners. And in the amen corner that quickly formed on the secular Right, commentators like Robert Novak and Pat Buchanan added that we had called the attack down on our heads not so much by our willful disobedience to divine law as by our manipulated obedience to Israel.

Oddly enough, however, within the Arab world itself there was much less emphasis on Israel as the root cause of the attacks than was placed on it by Buchanan's fellow paleoconservatives on the Right. As we have seen, even to Osama bin Laden, support of Israel ranked only third on a list of our "crimes" against Islam, and Israel itself was only fourth on a list of preferred targets for terrorist attack.

Not, to be sure, that Arabs everywhere—together with most non-Arab Middle Eastern Muslims like the Iranians—had given up their dream of wiping Israel off the map. To anyone who thought otherwise, Fouad Ajami of Johns Hopkins, an American who grew up as a Muslim in Lebanon, had this to say about the

Arab world's "great refusal" to accept Israel under any conditions whatsoever:

> The great refusal persists in that "Arab street" of ordinary men and women, among the intellectuals and the writers, and in the professional syndicates. . . . The force of this refusal can be seen in the press of the governments and of the oppositionists, among the secularists and the Islamists alike, in countries that have concluded diplomatic agreements with Israel and those that haven't.

Ajami emphasized that the great refusal remained "fiercest in Egypt," notwithstanding the peace treaty it had signed with Israel in 1978. It might have been expected, then, that the Egyptians would be eager to blame the widespread animus against the United States in their own country on American policy toward Israel, especially since Egypt, being second only to the Jewish state as a recipient of American aid, had a powerful incentive to explain away so ungrateful a response to the benevolent treatment it was receiving at our hands. But no. Only about two weeks before 9/11, Ab'd Al-Mun'im Murad, a columnist in *Al-Akhbar*, a daily newspaper sponsored by the Egyptian government, wrote:

> The conflict that we call the Arab-Israeli conflict is, in truth, an Arab conflict with Western, and particularly American, colonialism. The U.S. treats [the Arabs] as it treated the slaves inside the American continent. To this end, [the United States] is helped by the smaller enemy, and I mean Israel.

In another piece, the same writer expanded on this unusually candid acknowledgment:

> The issue no longer concerns the Israeli-Arab conflict. The real issue is the Arab-American conflict—Arabs must understand that the U.S. is not "the American friend"—and its task, past, present, and future, is [to impose] hegemony on the world, primarily on the Middle East and the Arab world.

Then, in a third piece, also published in late August 2001, Murad gave us an inkling of the reciprocal "task" he had in mind to be performed on America:

> The Statue of Liberty, in New York Harbor, must be destroyed because of . . . the idiotic American policy that goes from disgrace to disgrace in the swamp of bias and blind fanaticism. . . . The age of the American collapse has begun.

If this was the kind of thing we were getting from an Arab country that everyone regarded as "moderate," in radical states like Iraq and Iran nothing less would suffice than identifying America as the "Great Satan." As for the Palestinians, their contempt for America was hardly exceeded by their loathing of Israel. For example, the mufti—or chief cleric—appointed by the Palestinian Authority under Yasir Arafat had prayed that God would "destroy America," while the editor of a leading Palestinian journal proclaimed:

> History does not remember the United States, but it remembers Iraq, the cradle of civilization. . . . History remembers every piece of Arab land, because it is the bosom of human civilization. On the other hand, the [American] murderers of humanity, the creators of the barbaric culture and the bloodsuckers of nations, are doomed to death and destined to shrink to a microscopic size, like Micronesia.

The absence of even a word here about Israel showed that if the Jewish state had never come into existence, the United States would still have stood as an embodiment of everything that most of these Arabs considered evil. Indeed, the hatred of Israel was in large part a surrogate for anti-Americanism, rather than the reverse. Israel was seen as the spearhead of the American drive for domination over the Middle East. As such, the Jewish state was a translation of America into, as it were, Hebrew—the "little enemy," the "little Satan." To rid the region of it would thus be tantamount to cleansing an area belonging to Islam (*dar al-Islam*) of the blasphemous political, social, and cultural influences emanating from a barbaric and murderous force. But the force, so to speak, was with America, of which Israel was merely an instrument.

Although Buchanan and Novak were earlier and more outspoken in blaming 9/11 on American friendliness toward Israel, this idea was not confined to the Right or to the marginal precincts of paleoconservatism. On the contrary: while it first popped up on the Right, it thoroughly pervaded the radical Left and much of the soft Left, and it was even espoused, albeit in attenuated form, by a number of liberal centrists like the *Slate* columnist Mickey Kaus (who, as against those of us who argued that Israel was not the main issue, made a special point of insisting that it was, at least "partly"). For the moment, in fact, the blame-Israel-firsters were concentrated most heavily on the Left.

It was also on the Left, and above all in the universities, that their fraternal twins, the blame-America-firsters, were located. Yet Eric Foner, a professor of history at Columbia, risibly claimed that the ACTA report was misleading since the polls proved that there was "firm support" for the war among college students. "If our aim is to indoctrinate students with unpatriotic beliefs," Foner smirked, "we're obviously doing a very poor job of it."

But what Foner, as a historian, must have known but neglected to mention was that even at the height of the radical fevers on campuses in the 1960s, only a minority of students sided with the antiwar radicals. Still, even though they were in the majority, the nonradical students were unable to make themselves heard above the antiwar din, and whenever they tried, they were shouted down. This was how it was, too, on campuses after 9/11. There were, here and there, brave defiers of the academic orthodoxies. But mostly the silent majority remained silent, for fear of incurring the disapproval of their teachers, or even of being punished for the crime of "insensitivity."

Such, then, was the assault that began to be mounted within hours of 9/11 by the guerrillas-with-tenure in the universities, along with their spiritual and political disciples scattered throughout other quarters of our culture. Could this "tiny handful of aging Rip van Winkles," in the breezy brush-off by Hendrick Hertzberg in *The New Yorker*, grow into a force as powerful as the "jackal bins" of yesteryear? Was the upsurge of confidence in America and American virtue that spontaneously materialized on September 11 strong enough to withstand the jackal bins this time around?

Some who shared my apprehensions believed that if things went well on the military front, all would be well on the home front too. And that was how it appeared from the effect wrought by the spectacular success of the Afghanistan campaign, which (for a short spell) disposed of the "quagmire" theory and also dampened anti-war activity on at least a number of campuses. Nevertheless, the mopping-up operation in Afghanistan created an opportunity for more subtle forms of opposition to gain traction. There were complaints that the terrorists captured in Afghanistan and then sent to a special facility in Guantánamo were not being treated as regular prisoners of war. Never mind that as irregulars without uniforms caught on the battlefield they were not entitled to such treatment under the Geneva Convention (and would once have been summarily executed). Never mind, too, that they were accorded many more rights and privileges than regular German or Japanese prisoners of war enjoyed in World War II. In spite of all this, it kept being charged that the Bush administration was violating the Geneva Convention and abusing the inmates at Guantánamo.*

---

* A Belgian police official, after visiting Guantánamo in 2006, would call it "a model prison where people are treated better than in Belgian prisons." No wonder. By the time of this visit, the average detainee even in the maximum-security camp had gained eighteen pounds; excellent medical care was available, even including expensive advanced procedures such as colonoscopies (sixteen of which had been performed). Furthermore, as Robert Pollack of the *Wall Street Journal* would report, "detainees were being treated in accordance with the restrictive rules of the Army Field Manual, which bans all forms of coercive interrogation. . . . Not only does that mean no 'torture' is going on. Your average good-cop bad-cop routine isn't allowed. Cooperative detainees get rewards like movies. *Harry Potter* is one of their favorites." Nor would they "lack for [free] legal representation. A list of lead {pro bono} counsel . . . reads like a who's who of America's most prestigious law firms."

Around the same time, it began being alleged that the Patriot Act, which had been designed to ward off any further terrorist attacks at home, was posing a serious threat to civil liberties. To these allegations a good response would later be made by John Yoo, formerly an official in the Bush Justice Department and now a professor of law at Berkeley. Pointing to Lincoln's suspension of habeas corpus in the Civil War, Wilson's prosecution of individuals for seditious speech in World War I, and Roosevelt's internment of more than 100,000 Japanese American citizens in World War II, Yoo would write:

> Nothing like the infringement of civil liberties in past wars has occurred nor are they likely to under current law. . . . The question is not whether some imaginary perfect world of civil liberties has been destroyed, because we do not live in that world. Have security policies gone further than necessary? The Patriot Act is a modest effort to adapt existing surveillance tools and strategies to an enemy whose unprecedented methods demand that intelligence be gathered on some civilian activity.

Lanny Davis, a self-described civil libertarian who had served as special counsel in the Clinton White House, would agree with this judgment. Upon becoming a member of the Privacy and Civil Liberties Oversight Board set up by Congress to keep an eye on the Bush administration's surveillance policies, Davis found himself pleasantly surprised to discover "how careful the government is to protect our privacy while still protecting us from attacks."

As Yoo himself would acknowledge, and as Davis would surely have agreed, some people no doubt raised these allegations against the Patriot Act in good faith. But I would add that there was also no doubt that such issues could—and did—serve as a respectable cover for wholesale opposition to the entire war.

Another respectable cover was the charge that Bush was following a policy of "unilateralism." The alarm over this supposedly unheard-of outrage was first sounded by the chancelleries and chattering classes of Western Europe when Bush stated that, in taking the fight to the terrorists and their sponsors, we would prefer to do so with allies and with the blessing of the UN, but if necessary we would go it alone and without an imprimatur from the Security Council.

This was too much for the Europeans. Having duly offered us their condolences over 9/11, they could barely let a decent interval pass before going back into the ancient family business of showing how vastly superior in wisdom and finesse they were to the Americans, whose primitive character was once again on display in the "simplistic" ideas and crude moralizing of George W. Bush. Now they urged that our military operations end with Afghanistan and that we leave the rest to diplomacy in deferential consultation with the great masters of that recondite art in Paris and Brussels.

Taking its cue from these masters, the *New York Times*, along with many other publications ranging from the Center to the hard Left—and soon to be seconded by all the Democratic candidates in the 2004 presidential primaries except for Senator Joseph Lieberman—began hitting Bush for recklessness and overreaching. What we saw developing here was a broader coalition than the antiwar movement spawned by Vietnam had managed to put together, especially in its first few years. The antiwar movement then had been made up almost entirely of leftists and liberals, whereas this new movement was bringing together the whole of the hard Left, elements of the soft Left, and sectors of the American Right.

Thus, treading the path previously marked out by his colleague Mickey Kaus on the issue of Israel, Michael Kinsley of the soft Left allied himself with Pat Buchanan in bringing forth yet another respectable cover. This was to indict the president for evading the Constitution by proposing to fight undeclared wars. Meanwhile, the same charge was moving into the political mainstream through Democratic senators like Robert Byrd, Edward M. Kennedy, and Tom Daschle, though they also continued carrying on about quagmires and slippery slopes and "unilateralism."

I for one was certain that, as the military facet of World War

IV widened—with Iraq clearly being the next most likely front—
opposition not only would grow but would acquire enough assurance to dispense with any respectable covers. Which was to say
that it would be taken over by extremists and radicalized. About
this I would turn out to be right, while those who scoffed at the
"jackal bins" and the "aging Rip Van Winkles" as a politically insignificant bunch would turn out to be wrong. But even I never
imagined that the new antiwar movement would so rapidly arrive
at the stage of virulence it had taken years for its ancestors of the
Vietnam era to reach. Nor did I anticipate how closely the antiwar
playbook of that era would be followed and how successfully it
would be applied to Iraq, even though the two wars had nothing
whatever in common. This time, mainly because there was no
draft, there would be no student protesters and no massive street
demonstrations; instead, virtual demonstrations would be mounted
in cyberspace by the so-called netroots, and these, more suited to
the nature of the new technological age, would prove to be an all-
too-effective substitute.*

---

* In the definition offered by the online encyclopedia Wikipedia: "**Netroots** is a
recent term coined to describe *political activism* organized through *blogs* and other
online media. . . . The word is a portmanteau of *Internet* and *grassroots*, reflect-
ing the technological innovations that supposedly set netroots techniques apart
from other forms of political participation. In the United States, the term is used
mainly in left-wing circles."

CHAPTER SIX

VARIETIES OF
ANTI-AMERICANISM

POSSIBLE EXPLANATION of the great velocity achieved by the new antiwar movement was that, like the respectable critique immediately preceding it, the radical opposition was following the lead of European opinion. In this instance, encouragement and reinforcement came from the almost incredible degree of hostility to America that erupted in the wake of 9/11 all over the European continent, and most blatantly in France and Germany, and that metastasized in the run-up to the invasion of Iraq. If demonstrations and public opinion polls could be believed, huge numbers of Europeans loathed the United States so deeply that they were unwilling to side with it even against Saddam Hussein, one of the most tyrannical and murderous despots on earth.

As Nick Cohen of the London *Observer*, a self-described leftist who nevertheless supported the invasion of Iraq, would later write:

On 15 February 2003, about a million liberal-minded people marched through London to oppose the overthrow of a fascist regime. It was the biggest protest in British history, but it was dwarfed by the march to oppose the overthrow of a fascist regime in Mussolini's old capital of Rome, where about three million Italians joined what the Guinness Book of Records said was the largest anti-war rally ever. In Madrid, about 650,000 marched to oppose the overthrow of a fascist regime in the biggest demonstration in Spain since the death of General Franco in 1975. In Berlin, the call to oppose the overthrow of a facist regime brought demonstrators from 300 German towns and cities, some of them old enough to remember when Adolf Hitler ruled from the Reich Chancellery. In Greece, where the previous generation had overthrown a military junta, the police had to fire tear gas at leftists who were so angry at the prospect of a fascist regime being overthrown that they armed themselves with petrol bombs.

In France and Ireland, Cohen would continue, it was a bit different:

The French protests against the overthrow of a fascist regime went off without trouble. Between 100,000 and 200,000 French demonstrators stayed peaceful as they rallied in the Place de la Bastille, where in 1789 Parisian revolutionaries had stormed the dungeons of Louis XVI in the name of the universal rights of man.

In Ireland, Sinn Fein was in charge of the protests and produced the most remarkable spectacle of a remarkable day: a peace movement led by the IRA. Only in the newly liberated countries of the Soviet bloc were the demonstrations small and anti-war sentiment muted. . . .

The total numbers, Cohen would conclude, were staggering:

No one knows how many people demonstrated. The BBC estimated between 6 and 10 million, and anti-war activists tripled that, but no one doubted that these were history's largest coordinated demonstrations and that millions, maybe tens of millions, had marched to keep a fascist regime in power.

That so many Europeans would take such a position could not have been, and was not, foreseen by most Americans. However, it came—or at any rate should have come—as no surprise that the

Muslim world would overwhelmingly side with Saddam against the United States.

Unlike in Europe, where the attacks of 9/11 did elicit a passing moment of sympathy for the United States ("We Are All Americans Now," proclaimed a headline the next day in *Le Monde*, the leading leftist daily in Paris), in the realm of Islam the news of 9/11 brought dancing in the streets and screams of jubilation. Almost to a man, Muslim clerics in their sermons assured the faithful that in striking a blow against the "Great Satan," Osama bin Laden had acted as a jihadist, or holy warrior, in strict accordance with the will of God.

This could have been predicted from a debate on the topic, "Bin Laden—The Arab Despair and American Fear," that was televised on the Arabic-language network Al-Jazeera about two months before 9/11. Using "American Fear" in the title was a bit premature, since this was a time when very few Americans were frightened by Islamist terrorism, for the simple reason that scarcely any had ever heard of bin Laden or Al Qaeda. Be that as it may, at the conclusion of the program the host said to the lone guest who had been denouncing bin Laden as a terrorist: "I am looking at the viewers' reactions for one that would support your positions—but . . . I can't find any." He then cited "an opinion poll in a Kuwaiti paper showing that 69 percent of Kuwaitis, Egyptians, Syrians, Lebanese, and Palestinians think bin Laden is an Arab hero and an Islamic jihad warrior." And on the basis of the station's own poll, he also estimated that among all Arabs, "from the Gulf to the Ocean," the proportion sharing this view of bin Laden was "maybe even 99 percent."

Surely, then, the chairman of the Syrian Arab Writers Associations was speaking for hordes of his "brothers" in declaring shortly after 9/11 that

> when the twin towers collapsed . . . I felt deep within me like someone delivered from the grave; I [felt] that I was being carried in the air above the corpse of the mythological symbol of arrogant

American imperialist power. . . . My lungs filled with air, and I breathed in relief, as I had never breathed before.

If this was how the Arab/Muslim world largely felt about 9/11, what could have been expected from that world when the United States picked itself up off the ground—Ground Zero, to be exact—and began fighting back? What could have been expected was precisely what happened: another furious outburst of anti-Americanism. Only this time the outbursts were infused not by jubilation but by the desperate hope that the United States would somehow be humiliated. This hope was soon extinguished by the quick defeat of the Taliban regime in Afghanistan, but it was immediately rekindled by the way Saddam Hussein was standing up against America. Saddam had killed as many as a million Muslims in the war he had fought against Iran only a few years earlier, and he had slaughtered several hundred thousand Arabs in his own country and Kuwait. Obviously, however, to his Arab and Muslim "brothers" this was completely canceled out by his defiance of the United States.

Was there, perhaps, an element of the same twisted sentiment in the willingness of millions upon millions of Europeans to lend de facto aid and comfort to this monster? Of course, the claim was that most such people were neither pro-Saddam nor anti-American: all they wanted was to "give peace a chance." But this claim was belied by the slogans, the body language, the speeches, and the manifestos of the "peace" party. Though hatred of America may not have been universal among opponents of American military action, it was obviously very widespread and very deep. And though other considerations (pacifist sentiment, concern about civilian casualties, contempt for George W. Bush, faith in the UN, etc.) were at work, these factors had no trouble coexisting harmoniously with extreme hostility to the United States.

Thus, within two months of 9/11, a survey of influential people in twenty-three countries was undertaken by the Pew Research Center, the Princeton Survey Research Associates, and the *International Herald Tribune*. Here is how a British newspaper summarized the findings:

Did America somehow ask for the terrorist outrages in New York and Washington? . . . Most people of influence in the rest of the world . . . believe that, to a certain extent, the U.S. was asking for it. . . . From its closest allies, in Europe, to the Middle East, Russia, and Asia, a uniform 70 percent said people considered it good that after September 11 Americans had realized what it was to be vulnerable.

It would therefore seem that the Italian playwright Dario Fo, winner of the Nobel Prize for Literature in 1997, was more representative of European opinion than he may at first have appeared when spewing out the following sentiment:

> The great speculators wallow in an economy that every year kills tens of millions of people with poverty—so what is 20,000 [sic] dead in New York? Regardless of who carried out the massacre, this violence is the legitimate daughter of the culture of violence, hunger, and inhumane exploitation.

In France, a leading philosopher and social theorist, Jean Baudrillard, produced a somewhat different type of apologia for the terrorists of 9/11 and their ilk. This was so laden with postmodern jargon and so convoluted that it bordered on parody ("The collapse of the towers of the World Trade Center is unimaginable, but this does not suffice to make it a real event"). But Baudrillard's piece did at least contain a revealing confession:

> That we have dreamed of this event, that everyone without exception has dreamed of it . . . is unacceptable for the Western moral conscience, but it is still a fact. . . . Ultimately, they [Al Qaeda] did it, but we willed it.

Much the same idea, in even more straightforward terms, was espoused across the Channel by Mary Beard, a teacher of classics at Cambridge University, who wrote: "However tactfully you dress it up, the United States had it coming. . . . World bullies . . . will in the end pay the price." With this the highly regarded novelist

Martin Amis agreed. But Beard's old-fashioned English plainness evidently being a little too plain for him, Amis resorted to a bit of fancy continental footwork in formulating his own endorsement of the idea that America had been asking for it:

> Terrorism is political communication by other means. The message of September 11 ran as follows: America, it is time you learned how implacably you are hated. . . . Various national characteristics—self-reliance, a fiercer patriotism than any in Western Europe, an assiduous geographical incuriosity—have created a deficit of empathy for the sufferings of people far away.

What on earth was going on here? After 9/11, most Americans had gradually come to recognize that we were hated by the terrorists who had attacked us and by their Muslim cheerleaders, not for our failings and sins, but precisely for our virtues as a free and prosperous country. But why should we be hated by hordes of people living in other free and prosperous countries? In their case, presumably, it must be for our sins. And yet, whatever sins we might have committed, they were for certain not the ones of which the Europeans kept accusing us.

To wit: far from being a nation of overbearing bullies, we were humbly begging for the support of tiny countries we could easily have pushed around. Far from being "unilateralists," we were busy soliciting the gratuitous permission and the dubious blessing of the Security Council before taking military action against Saddam Hussein. Far from "rushing into war," we were spending months dancing a diplomatic gavotte in the vain hope of enlisting the help of France, Germany, and Russia. And so on, and so on, down to the last detail in the catalog.

What, then, was going on? An answer to this puzzling question that would eventually gain perhaps the widest circulation came from Robert Kagan of the Carnegie Endowment. In a catchy formulation that soon became famous, Kagan proposed that Americans were from Mars and Europeans were from Venus. Expanding on this formulation, he wrote:

On the all-important question of power—the efficacy of power, the morality of power, the desirability of power—American and European perspectives are diverging. Europe is turning away from power, or to put it a little differently, it is moving beyond power into a self-contained world of laws and rules and transnational negotiation and cooperation. It is entering a post-historical paradise of peace and relative prosperity, the realization of Kant's "Perpetual Peace." The United States, meanwhile, remains mired in history, exercising power in the anarchic Hobbesian world where international laws and rules are unreliable and where true security and the defense and promotion of a liberal order still depend on the possession and use of military might.

In developing his theory, Kagan got many things right and cast a salubrious light into many dark corners. But he also seemed to me to be putting the shoes of his theory on the wrong feet. Although I fully accepted Kagan's description of the divergent attitudes toward military power, I did not agree that the Europeans were already living in the future while the United States remained "mired" in the past. In my judgment, the opposite was closer to the truth.

The "post-historical paradise" into which the Europeans were supposedly moving struck me as nothing more than the web of international institutions that had been created at the end of World War II under the leadership of the United States in the hope that they would foster peace and prosperity. These included the United Nations, the World Bank, the World Court, and others. Then, after 1947, and again under the leadership of the United States, adaptations were made to the already existing institutions and new ones like NATO were added to fit the needs of World War III. With the victorious conclusion of World War III in 1989–90, however, the old international order became obsolete, and new arrangements tailored to a new era needed to be forged. But more than a decade elapsed before 9/11 finally made the contours of the "post–cold war era" clear enough for these new arrangements to begin being developed.

Looked at from this angle, the Bush Doctrine revealed itself as an extremely bold effort to break out of the institutional framework and the strategy constructed to fight the last war. But it was more: it also drew up a blueprint for a new structure and a new strategy to fight a different breed of enemy in a war that was just starting and that showed signs of stretching out into the future as far as the eye could see. Facing the realities of what now confronted us, Bush had come to the conclusion that few if any of the old instrumentalities were capable of defeating this new breed of enemy and that the strategies of the past were equally helpless before this enemy's way of waging war. To move into the future meant to substitute preemption for deterrence and to rely on American military might rather than the "soft power" represented by the UN and the other relics of World War III.

Examined from this same angle, the European justifications for resisting the Bush Doctrine—the complaints about "unilateralism," trigger-happiness, and the rest—were unveiled as mere rationalizations. Kagan correctly traced these rationalizations to a decline in the power of the Europeans:

> World War II all but destroyed European nations as global powers. . . . For a half-century after World War II, however, this weakness was masked by the unique geopolitical circumstances of the cold war. Dwarfed by the two superpowers on its flanks, a weakened Europe nevertheless served as the central strategic theater of the worldwide struggle between Communism and democratic capitalism. . . . Although shorn of most traditional measures of great-power status, Europe remained the geopolitical pivot, and this, along with lingering habits of world leadership, allowed Europeans to retain international influence well beyond what their sheer military capabilities might have afforded. Europe lost this strategic centrality after the cold war ended, but it took a few more years for the lingering mirage of European global power to fade.

So far, so good. Where I parted company with Kagan's analysis was over his acquiescence in the claim that the Europeans had in fact made the leap into the postnational, or postmodern, "Kantian paradise" of the future. To me it seemed clear that it was they, and not we Americans, who were "mired" in the past. They were fighting tooth and nail against the American effort to move into the future precisely because holding on to the ideas, the strategic habits, and the international institutions of the cold war would allow them to go on exerting "international influence well beyond what their sheer military capabilities might have afforded." It was George W. Bush—that "simplistic" moralizer and trigger-happy "cowboy," that flouter of international law and reckless unilateralist—who had possessed the wit to see the future and had summoned up the courage to begin crossing over into it.

But Bush was also a politician, and as such he felt it necessary to make some accommodation to the pressures coming at him both at home and from abroad. What this required was an occasional return visit to the past. On such visits, as when he would seek endorsements from the UN Security Council, he showed a polite measure of deference to those, again both at home and abroad, who insisted on reading the Bush Doctrine not as a blueprint for the future but as a reckless repudiation of the approach favored by the allegedly more sophisticated Europeans and their American counterparts. In Kagan's apt description of how the Europeans saw themselves:

> Europeans insist they approach problems with greater nuance and sophistication. They try to influence others through subtlety and indirection. . . . They generally favor peaceful responses to problems, preferring negotiation, diplomacy, and persuasion to coercion. They are quicker to appeal to international law, international conventions, and international opinion to adjudicate disputes. They try to use commercial and economic ties to bind nations together. They often emphasize process over result, believing that ultimately process can become substance.

None of this was new: the Europeans had made almost exactly the same claim of superior sophistication during the Reagan years. At that time—in 1983—it had elicited a definitive comment from Owen Harries (himself a member of the realist school who had been the head of policy planning in the Department of Foreign Affairs in Australia and the editor of the *National Interest* in America):

> When one is exposed to this claim of superior realism and sophistication, one's first inclination is to ask where exactly is the evidence for it. If one considers some of the salient episodes in the history of Europe in this century—the events leading up to 1914, the Versailles peace conference, Munich, the extent of the effort Europe has been prepared to make to secure its own defense since 1948, and the current attitude toward the defense of its vital interests in the Persian gulf—one is not irresistibly led to concede European superiority.

Two decades later, Harries as a realist would have his own grave reservations about the Bush Doctrine. But I had no hesitation in adding the "sophisticated" European opposition to it as the latest episode in the long string of disastrously mistaken judgments he had enumerated back in 1983.

But there was yet another, and even more ominous, aspect to this opposition that manifested itself in the demographic realities of Western Europe. For one thing, the birthrates of all the European countries were falling below—and in some cases far below—the 2.1 level required to prevent a decline in population. For another thing, Muslims were making up an ever-increasing proportion of this shrinking population. Yet instead of wishing to assimilate into the native culture of the West, most of the recent Muslim immigrants seemed to be rejecting it. Worse yet, they were becoming more and more susceptible to the appeal of the Islamofascists among them, and many of their children, along even with the native-born offspring of an earlier generation of Muslim immigrants, were following the same path. Thus, for example, the terrorist attacks in London on July 7, 2005, were carried out by Muslims born and bred in the United Kingdom.

Taken together, these two trends were seen by commentators like Bat Ye'or and Mark Steyn as a process whose end result would be the suicide of Europe as a bastion of Western civilization and its transformation into what they and others were beginning to call "Eurabia." But even in the short run, the large percentage of Muslim voters in every European country meant that politicians were being forced to cater to them, and this in turn meant that the "sophisticated" European opposition to the Bush Doctrine would be greatly reinforced by domestic political considerations.

All the more reason would there be, then, for the United States to forge ahead without waiting for permission from or the blessing of its erstwhile allies in Western Europe.

CHAPTER SEVEN

THE MAINSTREAM MEDIA

FOLLOWING UPON THE overthrow of the Taliban in Afghanistan, the astonishing success of the campaign to topple Saddam Hussein in Iraq made a hash of the skepticism of the many pundits who had been so sure that we had too few troops or were following the wrong battle plan. Instead of getting bogged down, as these pundits had predicted, our forces raced through the campaign in record time, and instead of tens of thousands of body bags being flown home, the casualties were numbered in the hundreds. As the military historian Victor Davis Hanson summarized what had transpired in Iraq:

> In a span of about three weeks, the United States military overran a country the size of California. It utterly obliterated Saddam Hussein's military hardware . . . and tore apart his armies. Of the approximately 110 American deaths in the course of the hostilities, fully a fourth occurred as a result of accidents, friendly fire, or peacekeeping mishaps rather than at the hands of enemy soldiers. The extraordinarily low ratio of total American casualties per number of U.S. soldiers deployed . . . is almost unmatched in modern military history.

But then came the aftermath of major military operations, and it turned out to be rougher than the Pentagon seemed to have expected. Thanks to the guerrilla insurgency mounted by a coalition of Saddam's Sunni loyalists, radical Shiite militias, and jihadists imported from Iran, Syria, and other Muslim countries, American soldiers continued to be killed. By any historical standard, our total losses were still, and would remain, amazingly low. But this did not prevent the antiwar movement from harping on the American "body count" and battening on it.

I had feared from the outset that the antiwar movement would grow and become radicalized with the extension of the Bush Doctrine from Afghanistan to Iraq, and so it did. I had also feared that the process would be helped along by the mainstream media, and this too came to pass. As our struggle in Iraq stretched from months into years, their "neutrality" more and more revealed itself as the partisanship it actually was: a virulent hostility to George W. Bush and a correlative wish to see the doctrine that bore his name discredited by an American defeat in Iraq.

An especially vivid exhibition of how such partisanship worked went on display the morning after a new Iraqi constitution had been ratified by fully 79 percent of the electorate, many of whom had defied threats of death in traveling to cast their votes. It was an inspiring sight and a giant step toward the democratization of a country that had only yesterday been subject to a murderous tyranny. Certainly this was how the election seemed to those of us who were rooting for the success of the American struggle to help plant the seeds of democracy in Iraq. But it was not how it seemed to the *Washington Post*, which saw fit to bury the story on page 13. As for the paper's front page on that day, the columnist Jeff Jacoby noted that it

was dominated by a photograph, stretched across four columns, of three daughters at the funeral of their father . . . who had died from injuries suffered during a September 26 bombing in Baghdad. Two accompanying stories, both above the fold, were headlined "Military Has Lost 2,000 in Iraq" and "Bigger, Stronger, Homemade Bombs Now to Blame for Half of U.S.

Deaths." A nearby graphic—"The Toll"—divided the 2,000 deaths by type of military service.

Far from being peculiar to the *Washington Post*, this kind of coverage of Iraq was part of an already established pattern. The Australian blogger Arthur Chrenkoff summed it up well:

> Death, violence, terrorism, precarious political situation, problems with reconstruction, and public frustration (both in Iraq and America) dominate, if not overwhelm, the mainstream media coverage and commentary on Iraq.

Concerned that he might have been exaggerating when he made this assertion on the basis of his "gut feeling," Chrenkoff decided to check it out more scientifically. So he did "a little tally" of the stories published or broadcast all over the world on a single average day (which happened to be January 21, 2005). Here were some of the numbers that, with the help of the Google News Index, he was able to report from that one day:

- 2,642 stories about Condoleezza Rice's confirmation hearings, in the context of the grilling she received over the administration's Iraq policy
- 1,992 stories about suicide bombings and other terrorist attacks
- 887 stories about prisoner abuse by British soldiers
- 216 stories about hostages currently being held in Iraq
- 761 stories reporting on activities and public statements of insurgents
- 357 stories about the antiwar movement and the dropping public support for involvement in Iraq
- 182 stories about American servicemen killed and wounded in operations
- 217 stories about concerns for the fairness and validity of the Iraqi election (low security, low turnout, etc.)
- 107 stories about civilian deaths in Iraq
- 123 stories noting Vice President Cheney's admission that he had underestimated the task of reconstruction

- 118 stories about complicated and strained relations between the United States and Europe
- 121 stories discussing the possibility of an American pullout
- 27 stories about the sabotage of the Iraqi oil infrastructure

As against all this, the good news made a pathetic showing:

- 16 stories about security successes in the fight against insurgents
- 7 stories about positive developments relating to elections
- 73 stories about the return to Iraq of stolen antiquities*

It was the same with the three major television networks. Thus, according to the eminent political scientist James Q. Wilson, reporting on a survey of the evening news programs on ABC, CBS, and NBC:

> Between Jan. 1 and Sept. 30, 2005, nearly 1,400 stories appeared on the ABC, CBS, and NBC evening news. More than half focused on the costs and problems of the war, four times as many as those that discussed the successes. About 40 percent of the stories reported terrorist attacks; scarcely any reported the triumphs of American soldiers and Marines. The few positive stories about progress in Iraq were just a small fraction of all the broadcasts.

Another survey also cited by Wilson came up with evidence of the steep decline in media support as the campaign in Iraq went on:

* Chrenkoff added: "Many stories are 'duplicates' of wire reports from AP, Reuters, and others, but that's precisely the point: if a negative story from the AP is picked up by hundreds of newspapers around the world, then the story's penetration of the global news market is much greater than another story published in just one local newspaper. This, by the way, cuts both ways: if a wire service writes a positive story, that [too] gets syndicated worldwide (in fact most of the 73 positive stories above about the return of stolen treasures are such duplicates)—except that it's quite rare for a news wire service to have a good-news story."

When the Center for Media and Public Affairs made a nonpartisan evaluation of network news broadcasts, it found that during the active war against Saddam Hussein, 51 percent of the reports about the conflict were negative. Six months after the land battle ended, 77 percent were negative; by the spring of 2006, 94 percent were negative. This decline in media support was much faster than during Korea or Vietnam.

Meanwhile, on the editorial and op-ed pages, the pundits, the academic theorists, and the armchair generals were denouncing the Bush Doctrine and/or blaming the incompetence of the president and his appointees for what they all took for granted was a complete disaster. But here there was a difference in that the charge of incompetence was also beginning to be hurled by supporters of the Bush Doctrine in general and of the invasion of Iraq in particular whose intention was not to declare defeat but to prod the administration into doing a better job. The most formidable of these was Eliot A. Cohen himself, who now expressed

a desire—barely controlled—to slap the highly educated fool who, having no soldier friends or family, once explained to me that mistakes happen in all wars, and that the casualties are not really all that high, and that I really shouldn't get exercised about them.

Reading this, I had a mixed response. On the one hand, I could see that this person might well have deserved a slap for being presumptuous toward a distinguished military historian, or for insensitivity in downplaying casualties when speaking to the father, as Cohen was, of an infantry officer on his way to Iraq. But being what Cohen would undoubtedly consider another educated fool, I could not help thinking that we did indeed need to be reminded that mistakes happen in all wars and that the casualties in this one were very low by any historical standard.

Worse yet from Cohen's point of view, I even had heretical thoughts about the mistakes that so exercised him and almost everyone else. The main such "mistake" was the Pentagon's alleged failure to give enough thought to what would happen once we got to Baghdad and therefore to make plans for dealing with the aftermath of the combat phase. Yet, contrary to this allegation, much thought was given to, and many plans were made for dealing with, horrors that everyone expected to happen and then, mercifully, did not. Among these were: house-to-house fighting to take Baghdad; the flight of one million or more refugees; the setting afire of the oil fields; and the immediate outbreak of a major civil war.

As for the insurgency, even if its dimensions had accurately been foreseen, it would still have been impossible to eliminate it in short order. To cite Eliot Cohen himself:

> If the insurgencies in Northern Ireland, Israel/Palestine, Sri Lanka, and Kashmir continue, what reason do we have to expect this one to end so soon?

A related group of alleged "mistakes" was actually made up of judgment calls, concerning which it was possible for reasonable people to differ. The most widely condemned of these—especially among supporters of the war on the Right—was that there were too few American "boots on the ground" to mount an effective campaign against the insurgency. Perhaps. And yet there was good reason to believe that the key factor in fighting a terrorist insurgency was not the number of troops deployed against it but rather the amount and quality of the intelligence that could be obtained from infiltrating its ranks and from questioning prisoners (a task made all the more difficult for us by the campaign here at home to define "torture" down to the point where it would become illegal to subject even a captured terrorist to generally accepted methods of interrogation).

Finally, there were "mistakes" that were at bottom choices between two evils—choices that had to be made when it was by no means obvious which was the lesser of the two. The best example here was the policy of "de-Baathification," adopted shortly after the toppling of Saddam. This led to a disbanding of the Iraqi army, which was dominated by members of the Sunni minority through whom Saddam had ruled and who were now putatively left with nothing to do but volunteer their services to the insurgency. Yet allowing Saddam Hussein's thugs to continue controlling the army would have embittered the Shiites and the other major segment of the population, the Kurds, both of whom had suffered greatly at the hands of the Sunnis. Was it self-evident that this would have been better for us or for Iraq?

However, even conceding for the sake of argument that every one of these accusations was justified, I was still ready to contend that they amounted to chump change when stacked up against the mistakes that were made in World War II—a war conducted by acknowledged giants like Franklin D. Roosevelt and Winston Churchill. Tim Cavanaugh of *Reason*, in a posting on the magazine's website, had recently offered a partial list of such blunders and the lives that were lost because of them:

American Marines were slaughtered at Tarawa because the pre-invasion bombardment of the island was woefully deficient. Hundreds of American paratroopers were killed by American anti-aircraft fire during landings in Italy—for that matter the entire campaign up the Italian boot was an obvious waste of time, resources, and lives that prevented the western Allies from getting seriously into the war until the middle of 1944. . . . In late 1944, Allied commanders failed to anticipate that the Germans would attack through Belgium despite their having done so in 1914 and 1940.

In brief, Cavanaugh concluded, "on any given week, World War II offered more fuck-ups and catastrophes than anything that has been seen in postwar Iraq."

As for casualties, Cohen's educated fool was just plain right. At the time, the number in Iraq had reached about 2,000, a figure which was certainly "not all that high" by comparison with the losses we suffered in past wars: in World War II, 405,399; in Korea, 36,574; in Vietnam, 58,209.

In spite of all this, the idea kept spreading that Iraq was already a lost cause. But it was not the picture of a lost cause that we were getting from a number of Iraqi bloggers and from the many letters written by American soldiers in the field that were finding their way onto the Internet. These close-range observers did not overlook the persistence of major problems, and they did not deny that there was still a long way to go before Iraq could become secure, stable, and democratic. But what seemed most important to them was the amazing progress that had already been made and was continuing to be made, even under the gun of Islamofascist terrorism, in building—from scratch—the political morale of a country ravaged by "post-totalitarian stress disorder," in setting up the institutional foundations of a federal republic, in getting the economy moving, and in reconstructing the physical infrastructure.

Why was there so little public awareness of all this progress? One young reporter, who proudly proclaimed his membership in the mainstream media, was only too happy to provide an explanation:

> As long as American soldiers are getting killed nearly every day, we're not going to be giving much coverage to the opening of multimillion-dollar sewage projects. American lives are worth more than Iraqi shit.

From its professed concern with American casualties, one might have imagined that this statement was worlds away from the hostility to American military power—and to America in general—that pervaded the radical Left in the 1960s and that in its milder liberal mutation constituted the post-Vietnam syndrome. And it was certainly true that the antiwar movement spawned by Vietnam had rarely had a tear to shed for the American lives that were being lost there. But the newfound tenderness toward our troops in Iraq did not in the least reflect a change in attitude toward the use of force by the United States. To the contrary, the relentless harping on American casualties by the mainstream media was part of an increasingly desperate effort to portray Iraq as another Vietnam: a foolish and futile (if not immoral and illegal) resort to military power in pursuit of a worthless (if not unworthy) goal.

Mark Twain once famously said that reports of his death were greatly exaggerated. So it was in the immediate aftermath of 9/11 with those predictions by some younger commentators that the hostility to America and especially American power represented by the Vietnam syndrome would now finally disappear from our political culture. As was evident from the coverage of Iraq in the mainstream media, such pronouncements were more than a little premature: the Vietnam syndrome was still alive and well. But equally apparent was that the reporters and editors to whom it was a veritable religion understood very clearly that success in Iraq *could* deal the Vietnam syndrome a mortal blow. Little wonder, then, that they so resolutely tried to ignore any and all signs of progress—or, when that became impossible, that they dismissed them as so much "shit."

CHAPTER EIGHT

ISOLATIONISTS
RIGHT AND LEFT

I N ADDITION TO the journalistic devotees of the Vietnam syndrome, our domestic insurgency was made up of three other groups to whom success in Iraq was equally threatening and on whose ideas the mainstream media greedily fed. Like the mainstream media, the members of these three schools of thought understood almost from the word go that the Bush Doctrine involved a repudiation of the ideas and policies to which they were respectively committed. Accordingly, all of them also realized that they stood to lose everything if the doctrine were ever generally judged to have passed the great test to which it had been put in Iraq. With so great a stake in its failure, they were unwilling even to entertain the possibility that more and better things were happening in Iraq, as well as in the broader Middle East, than were dreamed of in their various philosophies.

The first group was the isolationists. Although probably the least influential of the three, they existed on both the extreme Right and the extreme Left, and appealing as they did to a persistent impulse on both ends of the political spectrum, their take on Iraq still resonated beyond their own relatively small circles.

On the Right, their leading spokesman was Pat Buchanan. Once upon a time, he had been much admired by conservatives of all stripes (myself included) for the vigor and pungency with which he usually expressed the hard-line conservative consensus of the Reagan era. But with the end of the cold war, his thinking about international affairs had begun veering off in an entirely different direction.

The most blatant manifestation of this change was his opposition to the first Gulf War. The position he took on this issue surprised many people who still thought of him as the pugnacious hawk he had always been in the fight against communism. Yet it had already been foreshadowed by the loudly announced conversion to isolationism with which he had celebrated the victorious conclusion of World War III and on the basis of which he had challenged the elder George Bush in the Republican presidential primaries of 1992. It was not, moreover, some vague or general brand of isolationism that this most ferocious of cold warriors had decided to embrace; it was a particular strain with a name and a history of its own: America First.

The purpose of the original America First movement, founded in 1940, was in the short run to oppose American aid to the nations of Europe threatened by Nazi Germany and in the longer run to keep the United States from going to war against Hitler. Although the movement attracted a number of prominent left-wing isolationists (among them the socialist leader Norman Thomas and the historian Charles A. Beard), its main support came from the Right and included the notorious anti-Semitic demagogue Father Charles Coughlin, the "radio priest." But America First's biggest star by far was the great aviation hero Charles Lindbergh.

"In September 1941," wrote the historian Alonzo L. Hamby of Ohio University,

> Lindbergh made a speech that listed Jews, the British, and the Roosevelt administration as the three forces propelling the country toward war. . . . [He] made no reference to other ethnic groups (Polish-Americans, for example) who also favored war with Germany, and [he] seemed to assume that Jewish-Americans were in some sense or another aliens.

What was most extraordinary about Buchanan's insistence on using the name of the old America First movement in his run for the Republican presidential nomination in 1992 was his willingness—or was it eagerness?—to embrace these unsavory aspects of its history as well. When, in that same year, Governor L. Douglas Wilder of Virginia, in search of a jazzy slogan for his own abortive campaign for the Democratic nomination, also and independently hit upon the term "America First," he was clearly unaware of or had forgotten about these associations, and he dropped it as soon as they were called to his attention. Buchanan, by contrast, knew exactly what he was doing and even went out of his way to pluck on the original strings. Indeed, he might almost have been consciously echoing Lindbergh when he made the notorious announcement on one of his television shows that the Israelis and the American Jews were the only forces pushing the elder Bush toward war in the Persian Gulf.

Again like Lindbergh (who at least had had the excuse of knowing that the country was split down the middle on getting into another European war), Buchanan ignored all the other groups, adding up to a large majority of the population, who had backed the Gulf War, and yet again like Lindbergh, Buchanan insinuated that American Jews (Israel's "amen corner") were not full-fledged Americans. As if to belie his apologists, who insisted that he had not meant to say what he seemed to be saying, he returned to the same theme during his run for the presidency when he responded to a group of Jewish protesters by declaring, "This is a rally of Americans, by Americans, and for the good old U.S.A."

Instead, then, of trying to distance himself from the anti-Semitic associations of the old America First movement, Buchanan moved with all due deliberation in the opposite direction, and kept right on moving for the next ten years. By the time the Bush Doctrine was enunciated, the whiff of anti-Semitism emitted by his writings had become so strong that they helped to discredit the isolationist ideas that might otherwise have gained him an audience beyond the small cadre of his paleoconservative followers. An American success in Iraq—which he called the main "laboratory and proving ground" of the neoconservative foreign policy Bush had "imposed on Ronald Reagan's party"—threatened to marginalize him even further. On the other hand, if Buchanan's ideas about the American role in the world were to be vindicated by a failure in Iraq, their anti-Semitic emanations might no longer be so great an obstacle to the expansion of his influence. For anti-Semitism disguised as anti-Zionism (and often not bothering to disguise itself at all) had been making a strong comeback after being banished from respectable society since 1945, when knowledge of the Holocaust had revealed where this most ancient of bigotries could end if permitted to go unchecked.

No wonder, then, that Buchanan began declaring, almost from the first day, that the operation in Iraq was doomed. Nor was it any wonder that he went on to pounce gleefully on every bit of bad news as further evidence of its dismal failure.

In this effort, the isolationists of the hard Left, exactly like their forebears in the late 1930s who had joined the America First committee and fought against the country's entry into World War II, made common cause with the Buchananites at the other end of the political spectrum. No matter that the isolationism of the Left stemmed from the conviction that America was bad for the rest of the world, whereas the isolationism of the Right was based on the belief that the rest of the world was bad for America. Even so, the two streams were able to converge and to flow smoothly into the same channel of fierce opposition to everything Bush had been doing in response to 9/11.

Buchanan's counterpart on the Left was Noam Chomsky. Chomsky's academic expertise lay in the field of linguistics, where he was regarded as a major figure—a reputation that did him no harm when he began writing about politics in the late 1960s. He also drew on his academic training to create an impression of scrupulous reasoning and meticulous scholarship; on the surface his political articles bore all the marks of sober scholarly discourse, including—always including—large numbers of footnotes. But under this veneer of reasonableness streamed a steady series of savage attacks on the war in Vietnam and everything and everyone connected with it.

Almost immediately these articles, mostly appearing in the *New York Review of Books*, brought him into great prominence. But at some point in the early 1970s, the extremism of his hatred of America ("the torture and political-murder capital of the world") and his equally passionate detestation of Israel (second only to America in torture and political murder) made him a liability to the *New York Review*, which was then trying to inch away from its own early extremism. Nor, as the passions aroused by Vietnam had begun to cool, could he hold on to the audience that had once devoured his every word. In this changing climate, moreover, it did not help that Chomsky, even though he sometimes called himself a libertarian anarchist, repeatedly rushed to apologize for or side with any totalitarian despot, whether Communist or fascist and no matter how murderous, provided only that the despot in question was ranged against the United States. To the consternation even of some formerly devoted admirers, this included Pol Pot, who had slaughtered one-third or more of his own people in setting up a Communist regime in Cambodia. As a result of all this, Chomsky, too, like Buchanan, was increasingly relegated to the margins and largely forgotten.

After 9/11, however, and unlike Buchanan, Chomsky found a newly receptive audience and one bigger than ever. Arch Puddington of Freedom House summed it up in an article in *Commentary*:

> *9/11*, a pamphlet-sized book of responses to questions from foreign journalists, sold over 300,000 copies in 23 languages. According to one survey, Chomsky is the most cited living author, and the eighth most cited of all time (just behind Freud). His speeches draw packed houses. At the World Social Forum, an annual gathering of the anti-globalist movement, he is a featured personality. The current generation of young leftists treat Chomsky

as a celebrity, and pay him the kind of homage normally reserved for rock stars or cult icons. He is the subject of several reverential documentary films, which depict him as an isolated voice of truth against a corrupt and warmongering establishment, and he has even inspired a one-man theater work, *The Loneliness of Noam Chomsky*.

Nor was this the whole of it:

> Chomsky's enhanced influence is reflected in the respect he now commands in the mainstream American press. Formerly ignored or treated as something of a fringe figure, he is sought out these days by major newspapers and is occasionally asked to write op-eds on the war on terror. His most recent book . . . was deferentially reviewed in the daily press and in journals of opinion, and he has been the subject of lengthy profiles in the *Washington Post* and *The New Yorker.*

Such were the rewards Chomsky reaped for contending that the United States had brought the terrorist attacks down upon its own head; for his general belief that America was the greatest force for evil in the world; and for his denunciations of our response to 9/11 as a cover for carrying on with the criminal imperialism of which he had been accusing the United States practically from the moment of his birth. Thus, only days after 9/11 he delivered a lecture in India in which he announced that the United States was at that moment serenely preparing to commit "some sort" of genocide in Afghanistan:

> What will happen, we don't know, but plans are being made and programs implemented on the assumption that they may lead to the death of several million people in the next few months, very casually, with no comment, no particular thought about it.

There was no doubt that so long as his lungs held out, and no matter what might happen in Iraq, Chomsky would go on railing in the same terms against America. But it was equally certain that if the campaign in Iraq were to succeed, he would lose his newly found mass audience and be returned to the narrow sectarian ghetto from which he had been able to break out after 9/11. Not a pleasant prospect, even for a fanatic like him.

CHAPTER NINE

LIBERAL INTERNATIONALISTS

THE SECOND OF the three schools of thought feeding the domestic insurgency was liberal internationalism. Like the isolationists, the members of this school—whose most sophisticated spokesmen included Stanley Hoffmann of Harvard, Charles A. Kupchan of the Council on Foreign Relations, and G. John Ikenberry of Georgetown—had a life-and-death stake in the outcome in Iraq. But unlike the isolationists, they were in good standing within the old foreign policy establishment. As such, they were comfortably housed in the political science departments of the universities and in bodies like the Council on Foreign Relations, the Brookings Institution, and the Carnegie Endowment; they were also the dominant force within the populous community of nongovernmental organizations (NGOs). What characterized them was a virtually religious commitment to negotiations as the best, or indeed the only, way to resolve conflicts; an unshakable faith in the UN; and a corresponding squeamishness about military force.

So stubborn, indeed, was their faith in the UN that nothing seemed to shake their view of it as the great instrument of collective security—not even the report of its own "High-Level Panel on Threats, Challenges, and Changes," which had just acknowledged that the organization was marked by "an unwillingness to get serious about preventing deadly violence." Nor did they give up their belief in the UN as the moral arbiter of the entire planet when it was revealed that billions of dollars flowing from the oil-for-food program, which was supposed to help feed the people of Iraq, wound up instead in the pockets of Saddam Hussein, in the coffers of countries, like France, with which he was doing business, and in the Swiss bank accounts of certain UN officials who helped direct this corrupt financial traffic.

Under Jimmy Carter (whose secretary of state, Cyrus R. Vance, was a devout member of this school) and to a lesser extent under Bill Clinton, the liberal internationalists had been at the very heart of American foreign policy. But while George W. Bush had thrown a rhetorical bone or two in their direction and had even done them the kindness of making a few ceremonial bows to the UN, he was for all practical purposes writing off the liberal internationalist school as a relic of the past. Nor was he coy about this. As he declared in his speech at West Point on June 1, 2002:

> We cannot defend America and our friends by hoping for the best. We cannot put our faith in the word of tyrants, who solemnly sign nonproliferation treaties, and then systematically break them.

The liberal internationalists were not slow to pick up on what statements like this held in store for them. While Kupchan thought that a number of other forces had already weakened their position before, it was, he said flatly, "the election of George W. Bush [that] sounded the death-knell for liberal internationalism" (defined by him as "a moderate, centrist internationalism that manages the international system through compromise, consensus, and international institutions"). Ikenberry, on the other hand, blamed Bush alone:

> [A] set of hard-line, fundamentalist ideas have taken Washington by storm and provided the intellectual rationale for a radical

post–11 September reorientation of American foreign policy. . . . [This] is not leadership but a geostrategic wrecking ball that will destroy America's own half-century-old international architecture.

What Ikenberry did not say was that, thanks to the workings of this "wrecking ball," the liberal internationalists had been reduced to a domestic echo chamber for the French and the Germans. All they seemed able to do was count the ways in which the "unilateral" invasion of Iraq had, in Ikenberry's words, done "damage to the country's international position—its prestige, credibility, security partnerships, and the goodwill of other countries." Since they refused even to consider whether 9/11 demanded a "reorientation"—whether, that is, it had demonstrated that, as one foreign observer put it, "the tools and doctrines of the [old] system had outlived their utility" and needed to be replaced with a "new set of rules for managing the emerging threats to international security"*—they could hope for nothing better than a reversion to the status quo ante.

This dream, mused Stanley Hoffmann, could yet come true through the scuttling of the Bush Doctrine via a withdrawal from Iraq that

> would bring about a reconciliation with friends and allies shocked by Washington's recent unilateralism and repudiation of international obligations, and thus do much to restore . . . American credibility and "soft power" in the world.

As against Hoffmann, neither Ikenberry nor Kupchan envisaged so rosy a future for their common creed, even in the exceedingly unlikely event that the Bush Doctrine were to be abandoned.

* The foreign observer was Raja Mohan, professor of South Asian studies at Jawaharlal Nehru University in New Delhi, in a piece in the *Wall Street Journal* explaining why India, unlike Germany, France, and the liberal internationalists in the United States, was an enthusiastic supporter of the Bush Doctrine.

If, however, the doctrine were to be vindicated by Iraq, they all feared—and rightly so—that it would be almost impossible, in Kupchan's words, to "bring the U.S. back to a liberal brand of internationalism." Which, of course, meant that its exponents would lose their comfortable lodgings within the old foreign policy establishment.

Naturally, then, the liberal internationalists made common cause with the isolationists in the domestic insurgency against the Bush Doctrine. With more than a little help from their disciples and allies in the media, they worked night and day to prove that it was failing in Iraq or even that it had already failed.

CHAPTER TEN

REALISTS

O F ALL THE groups making up the domestic insurgency against the Bush Doctrine, the one with the most to lose was the realists, who were even more centrally located in the precincts of the old foreign policy establishment than their liberal internationalist neighbors.

The realist school took its name from the German *Realpolitik*, which did not in itself convey the impression, as the English name did, that it was necessarily more in tune with reality than other perspectives: it might or might not be, depending on the circumstances. To be sure, its German progenitors would never admit to any such limitation in their theory, and neither did the two refugees from Germany, Hans J. Morgenthau and Henry Kissinger, who brought that theory with them to America. To both Morgenthau and Kissinger, the supposedly discredited idealism of Woodrow Wilson was still alive and well, and it was infecting American foreign policy with a dangerous naïveté. This, beginning in the 1950s, they set out to correct with a series of books and articles making the theoretical case for realism. Actually, because Wilsonianism had much less influence than they imagined on the practice of American foreign policy, there was commensurately less need than they thought for a corrective. But they still made a big splash, perhaps because, like Molière's M. Jourdain, who had been speaking prose all his life without knowing it, the American foreign policy establishment was happy to learn that it had, all unawares, been putting a profound philosophical theory into practice.

The theory was based on two related precepts. The first was that in international affairs the great desideratum was stability, which could be achieved only through a proper balance of power. Following from this was a very old principle, going all the way back to the arrangements of the sixteenth century that grew out of the Treaty of Westphalia allowing for more or less peaceful co-existence among perennially warring Catholic and Protestant principalities. In its original form this principle was expressed in the Latin motto *cuius regio eius religio* (the religion of the ruler is the religion of the region). Translated into secular terms, it held that the internal character of a sovereign state was strictly its own affair, and only the actions it took beyond its own borders were the business of any other state.

In contrast to the liberal internationalists, the realists were not in the least squeamish about the use of force. But under the dictates of their basic principles, force was justified only in repelling another state's aggressive effort to upset a previously stable balance of power, while to make war in order to institute "regime change" was almost always both wrong and foolish. A good example of these dictates at work—to single it out yet again—was the first Gulf War, when George W. Bush's father used force to undo Saddam Hussein's invasion of Kuwait but stopped short of removing him from power in Iraq.

Until 9/11, the realists undoubtedly represented the dominant school of thought in the world of foreign policy, with all others considered naive or dangerous or both (though a patronizing pass might occasionally be given to the liberal internationalists). It would not be going too far to say that for just about everyone of any great importance in that world, whether as a theorist or a practitioner, the realist perspective was axiomatic. And being, as it were, the default position, it was almost automatically adopted by George W. Bush, too, in his pre-9/11 incarnation. But on 9/11,

Bush's more or less reflexive realism took so great a hit that it collapsed in flames just as surely as did the twin towers.

Bush made no secret of his repudiation of realism, and he did not pussyfoot around it:

> For decades, free nations tolerated oppression in the Middle East for the sake of stability. In practice, this approach brought little stability and much oppression, so I have changed this policy.

That took care of the first guiding precept of the realist perspective. And (in another passage I quoted earlier in a different context) Bush was equally forthright—almost brutal—in giving the back of his hand to the realist prohibition against using force to transform the internal character of other states:

> Some who call themselves realists question whether the spread of democracy in the Middle East should be any concern of ours. But the realists in this case have lost contact with a fundamental reality: America has always been less secure when freedom is in retreat; America is always more secure when freedom is on the march.

Farewell, then, as well to the Westphalian system of *cuius regio eius religio*.

What Bush was declaring here was a revolutionary change in the rules of the international game. But it was not until Iraq came to the fore that the realists grasped the full significance of this change. The reason was that the invasion of Afghanistan amounted only to a partial application of the new doctrine. Because the terrorists who had attacked us were based in Afghanistan and were protected and supported by the Taliban regime ruling that country, going after it did not constitute a preemptive strike. It represented, rather, a conventional retaliation against an unconventional aggression: they hit us and we hit back.

Being nothing really new, the invasion itself was not opposed in principle by the realists (even though some of them considered it crazy to think that we could win where so many other armies—most recently the Russians—had come a cropper). But the operation in Afghanistan did begin to conflict in principle with the realist perspective when it went beyond toppling the Taliban regime to sponsoring a replacement government pledged to democratization.

Still, the main criticism leveled by the realists at this point took a prudential form: our political objective, they said, was even more foolhardy than our military effort. This suggested that they were slower than the liberal internationalists in fully grasping what Bush was throwing at them. Probably unable to imagine that he could possibly be serious when he talked about reshaping the political character of the entire region, they seemed to have consoled themselves with the notion that Afghanistan was just a one-shot overreaction to 9/11.

If so, they were soon to be stripped of this cold comfort by the invasion of Iraq. And even then, it still took another while before the realists felt the full force of the gale being whipped up by George W. Bush. What caused the additional delay was the almost exclusive focus of the debate over Iraq on weapons of mass destruction.

When Bush charged Saddam Hussein with refusing to give up his weapons of mass destruction, he was (as we will see in much greater detail later on) relying in good faith on what the CIA—and every other intelligence agency in the world—assured him was the case. He was also acting in good faith when he warned that Saddam might put such weapons into the hands of terrorists and when he then invoked this danger in an advance justification of the new policy of preemption ("If we wait for threats to fully materialize, we will have waited too long").

But there would be a heavy price to pay for placing so much stress on the issue of WMD. Not only did the failure to find them retrospectively injure the case for invading Iraq; perhaps even more injurious was that the emphasis on WMD obscured the long-range strategic rationale for the invasion. For while the immediate objective was indeed to disarm Saddam Hussein, the larger one was to press on with "draining the swamps"—whether created by religious despots, as in Afghanistan, or by secular tyrants, as in Iraq—that were in Bush's view the breeding grounds of terrorism in the greater Middle East. Nor could those swamps be drained only by strong-arming the regimes under which they had been festering. It was also necessary in this view to replace these regimes with elected governments that would work to fulfill the hopes of "the peoples of the Islamic nations [who] want and deserve the same freedoms and opportunities as people in every nation."

All this pretty much disappeared from the debate over Iraq in the months before the invasion. Nevertheless, it gradually sank in among the realists that they had been wrong in dismissing Afghanistan as a one-shot affair and in thinking that disarming Saddam had been the be-all and end-all of the invasion of Iraq. Hard though it was for them, they finally had to face up to the incredible fact that Bush had not just been making rhetorical noises when he said that his ultimate strategic aim was to push all the states in the greater Middle East—every last one of them—toward democracy.

Worse yet, there was no dissuading him by argument, not even when close advisers of his father like Brent Scowcroft and James Baker—the former having been the elder Bush's national security adviser and the latter his secretary of state—were telling him that it was a mistake to invade Iraq. These realists were just as convinced as the paleoconservatives that Bush had been brainwashed by the neoconservative ideologues who had wormed their way into his mind, and this, they thought, was why he refused to recognize that by far the most important obstacle to solving all our problems in the Middle East was not Saddam Hussein but Ariel Sharon. So thoroughly brainwashed had he been by the neocons that he even remained calmly impervious to the objection that pursuing his new doctrine of democratization would destabilize the region (maddeningly, he responded that this was exactly what he *wanted* to do) and would also increase rather than lessen the danger of terrorism.

An interesting wrinkle in the story of the realist offensive against the Bush Doctrine was that it did not enlist the services of Henry Kissinger, the universally acknowledged leader of that school. Most of his disciples—including such prominent former assistants of his in the Nixon and Ford administrations as Scowcroft and Lawrence Eagleburger (later to become secretary of state himself for a short spell under the first George Bush)—lined up against the invasion of Iraq. But Kissinger himself, after hesitating a bit, came out in favor of using force against Saddam, and once the battle had begun, he was adamant about the need to stay the course. In sharp contrast to his less flexible students, Kissinger understood that what was at stake in the greater Middle East was American credibility and that the loss of this credibility would constitute the worst imaginable threat to the very stability that realists were supposed to pursue.*

Given his special take on Iraq—and even though he remained deeply skeptical about the short- or even medium-term prospects for democracy there and in the region at large—Kissinger did not and would not add his voice to the campaign against the Bush Doctrine mounted by other realists in the innumerable articles and books that came pouring out of them.** These polemics, like those of the liberal internationalists, were on the whole more restrained in tone—more patronizing than hysterical—than the ravings of the isolationists, but in substance and underneath the surface they were no less apocalyptic.

---

* Later, in opposing an American withdrawal from Iraq, Kissinger would invoke another traditionally "realist" argument, writing that our forces were not in Iraq "as a favor to its government or as a reward for its conduct. They are there as an expression of the American national interest to prevent the Iranian combination of imperialism and fundamentalist ideology from dominating a region on which the energy supplies of the industrial democracies depend."

** It may also be that Kissinger's skepticism about the Wilsonian side of the Bush Doctrine was tempered by his ability—rare among realists—to appreciate the great appeal of Wilsonianism: "[W]henever America has faced the task of constructing a new world order, it has returned in one way or another to Woodrow Wilson's precepts. . . . In Wilsonianism was incarnate the central drama of America on the world stage."

This came through with great clarity in a long and highly sympathetic survey of books attacking the Bush Doctrine that were produced by a mixed bag of realists and liberal internationalists who mostly resided in the academy.* Entitled "A Dissenter's Guide to Foreign Policy" and published in *World Policy Journal*, the survey was written by David C. Hendrickson, a professor of political science at Colorado College and a member of the Coalition for a Realistic Foreign Policy.

Hendrickson began by implicitly placing the things America had done under George W. Bush on a par with the "iniquities" of the Soviet Union under Stalin, from "the horrors of collectivization, the show trials, the devouring of the children of the Revolution in purges and assassinations," and up through "the Nazi-Soviet pact of 1939." For just as all this caused many Communists elsewhere to lose their faith in the benevolence of the Soviet Union, so, to the realists and the liberal internationalists surveyed by Hendrickson,

> the sheer enormity of what the Bush administration was attempting provoked a fundamental reevaluation of the belief that the United States was essentially, and despite imperfections, a tremendous force for good in the world. For them, as indeed for this reviewer, that proposition is now in grave doubt.

It did not occur to these opponents of the Bush Doctrine that if, because of its "unholy propensities," the end of America as a force for good was truly at hand, it would arrive in the form of an attack by terrorists armed with weapons of mass destruction. Nor did they stop to consider that there would be a much greater likelihood of such an attack if these "unholy propensities" were prevented from working themselves out than if they were allowed to take their course. But what must certainly have entered their minds was

---

* They included, among several others, *America Unbound: The Bush Revolution in American Foreign Policy* by Ivo Daalder and James M. Lindsay; *Fear's Empire: War, Terrorism, and Democracy* by Benjamin R. Barber; and *Rogue Nation: American Unilateralism and the Failure of Good Intentions* by Clyde Prestowitz.

that if these same "unholy propensities" were to succeed, realists like themselves (no less than the liberal internationalists) would be confronted with the impending end of *their* world. In the unkindest cut of all, their ideas would come to be dismissed as, precisely, unrealistic, and their standing would suffer a possibly fatal blow.

Before November 2, 2004, some realists had feared that Bush's reelection would, in Hendrickson's words, "confirm and ratify the revolutionary changes he has introduced to U.S. strategy." But once that dreaded event had occurred, they switched their hopes of averting the apocalypse to another possible outcome that some of them had already envisaged before November 2: namely, that "once revolutionary zeal collides with hard reality . . . the Bush policies . . . will end in tears."

Two years later, another realist, Philip Gordon of the Brookings Institution, would conclude that this was already coming to pass. Unlike virtually all his colleagues in the old foreign policy establishment who simply ignored the achievements of the Bush Doctrine, Gordon (perhaps feeling magnanimous in victory) was willing to acknowledge a few of them, including

> successful elections in Iraq and Afghanistan, a revolution in Lebanon followed by Syrian withdrawal, nuclear disarmament in Libya, and steps toward democracy elsewhere in the world.

One might have thought that this record would give Gordon pause, and one might also have thought that for the good of this country he would hope for more of the same. But no: what he most feared was "renewed progress in these areas." Why? Because further progress

> could give new force to the idea that a determined United States can transform the world and new arguments to those who believe that Bush should not waver in the promotion of his doctrine.

Better, in other words, for the United States to suffer defeat than for the Bush Doctrine to pull a Lazarus on Gordon and his colleagues, and then return to pursuing its hubristic goal of democratizing the entire Middle East.

Though they would all hotly deny it, it seemed clear that Hendrickson and Gordon, like many of their fellow realists and along with most liberal internationalists, were rooting for an American defeat as the only way to save their worldview from winding up on the ash heap of history.

The same thing could be said about no less prominent a figure than Zbigniew Brzezinski. Brzezinski had left the academy in 1976 to serve as Jimmy Carter's national security adviser, and with Carter's defeat at the hands of Ronald Reagan in 1980, he had returned whence he came and was now a professor again, in which capacity he wrote article after article excoriating the Bush Doctrine and all its works. In one typical example of these, a piece entitled "American Debacle," he began by accusing George W. Bush of "suicidal statecraft," went on to pronounce the intervention in Iraq (along with everything else this president had done) a total disaster, and ended by urging an early withdrawal of our troops from that hopeless battle.

Reading this piece, I shook my head in wonder at its sheer shamelessness. For here was George W. Bush being accused of "suicidal statecraft" by, of all people, the man who in the 1970s had helped shape a foreign policy that had emboldened the Iranians to seize American hostages while his boss in the Oval Office had stood impotently by for over a year before finally authorizing a rescue operation so inept that it had only compounded our national humiliation. And where was Brzezinski—famous at the time and admired by many (including me) for his implacable anticommunism—when the president he served congratulated us on having overcome our "inordinate fear of communism"? Where was Brzezinski—known far and wide for his hard-line determination to resist Soviet expansionism—when Cyrus Vance, the then secretary of state, had declared that the Soviet Union and the United States shared "similar dreams and aspirations," and when Carter himself had complacently informed us that containment was no longer necessary? And how was it that, despite daily meetings with Brzezinski, Carter had remained so blind to the nature of the Soviet regime that the invasion of Afghanistan had, as he himself put it, "made a more dramatic change in my own opinion of what the Soviets' ultimate goals are than anything they've done in the previous time I've been in office"? Had the cat gotten Brzezinski's tongue in the three years leading up to that invasion—the same tongue he now saw fit to wag with such brazen confidence at George W. Bush?*

But even if Brzezinski's record over the past thirty years did not disqualify him from dispensing advice on how to conduct American foreign policy, this diatribe against Bush would by itself have been enough. For here he looked over the Middle East, and what did he see? He saw the United States being "stamped as the imperialistic successor to Britain and as a partner of Israel in the military repression of the Arabs." This might not be fair, he covered himself by adding, but not a single word did he utter to indicate that the British had *created* the very despotisms the United States was now trying to replace with democratic regimes, or that George W. Bush was the first American president to have come out openly for a Palestinian state.

Again Brzezinski looked over the Middle East, and what did he see? He saw the treatment of captured terrorists causing the loss of America's "moral standing" as a "country that has stood tall" against "political repression, torture, and other violations of human rights." And that was all he saw—quite as though we had never liberated Afghanistan from the theocratic tyranny of the Taliban, or Iraq from the fascist despotism of Saddam Hussein. But how, after all, when it came to standing tall against "political repression, torture, and other violations of human rights," could such achievements compare with a sanctimonious lecture by Jimmy Carter followed by the embrace of one Third World dictator after another?

---

* As Thomas Joscelyn reminded us, Brzezinski had also wagged it at Ronald Reagan: "If present trends continue," he wrote in 1981, "American foreign policy is likely to be in a state of general crisis by the spring of 1982 . . . causing the global position of the United States to be placed in jeopardy."

Then for a third time Brzezinski looked over the Middle East, and what did he see? He saw more and more sympathy for terrorism, and more and more hatred of America, being generated throughout the region by our actions in Iraq, and in this context, too, that was all he could see. About the momentous encouragement that our actions had given to the forces of reform that never dared act or even speak up before, he was completely silent, though it was a phenomenon that even so inveterate a hater of America as the Lebanese dissident Walid Jumblatt had found himself compelled to recognize. Thus, only a few months after declaring that "the killing of U.S. soldiers in Iraq is legitimate and obligatory," Jumblatt suddenly woke up to what those U.S. soldiers had actually been doing for the world in which he lived:

> It's strange for me to say it, but this process of change has started because of the American invasion of Iraq. I was cynical about Iraq. But when I saw the Iraqi people voting [in January 2005], 8 million of them, it was the start of a new Arab world.

The Egyptian democratic activist Saad Eddin Ibrahim, who, like Jumblatt, originally opposed the invasion of Iraq, had said much the same thing:

> Those [in the Middle East] who believe in democracy and civil society are finally actors . . . [because the invasion of Iraq] has unfrozen the Middle East, just as Napoleon's 1798 expedition did. Elections in Iraq force the theocrats and autocrats to put democracy on the agenda, even if only to fight against us. Look, neither Napoleon nor President Bush could impregnate the region with political change. But they were able to be midwives.*

---

* In the wake of the war between Hezbollah and Israel in 2006, Ibrahim would undergo a change of heart about Bush, whom he would in effect accuse of failing to nurture the offspring he had helped bring into being. But since a midwife is not a nurse or a parent, his new position did not cancel out his original judgment. Moreover, it remained to be seen whether he would hold on to it indefinitely or alter his position again.

Nor were such changes confined to the political sphere. According to a report in *The Economist*, a revulsion against terrorism was beginning to spread among Muslim clerics, including some who, like the secular Jumblatt, had only recently applauded its use against Americans:

> Moderate Muslim clerics have grown increasingly concerned at the abuse of religion to justify killing. In Saudi Arabia, numerous preachers once famed for their fighting words now advise tolerance and restraint. Even so rigid a defender of suicide attacks against Israel . . . as Yusuf Qaradawi, the star preacher of the popular al-Jazeera satellite channel, denounces bombings elsewhere and calls on the perpetrators to repent.

The late Senator George Aiken of Vermont once proposed that we declare victory in Vietnam and then get out, but what Brzezinski wanted to do was declare defeat in Iraq and then get out. This, he mysteriously assured us (as Stanley Hoffmann had done earlier), would help restore "the legitimacy of America's global role." Of course, being defeated would do no such thing for America, any more than it had done in the wake of our ignominious withdrawal from Vietnam. On the other hand, by helping to restore the legitimacy of Brzezinski's ideas about America's global role, which would otherwise sink into oblivion, it would certainly do a lot for *him*.

Brzezinski's worldview could be described as realism mixed with a dash of liberal internationalism. In this, as in being a Democrat, he differed somewhat from his fellow former national security adviser, the Republican Brent Scowcroft, whose own commitment to the realist perspective was pure and unadulterated. But in spite of this divergence, the two men were at one in regarding the war in Iraq as a calamitous distraction from the really important business to which we should have been attending in the Middle East—namely, the conflict between Israel and the Palestinians. To quote again from the article Scowcroft published some months before the invasion of Iraq:

Possibly the most dire consequence [of attacking Saddam] would be the effect in the region. The shared view in the region is that Iraq is principally an obsession of the U.S. The obsession of the region, however, is the Israeli-Palestinian conflict. If we were seen to be turning our backs on that bitter conflict, there would be an explosion of outrage against us.

Scowcroft would stick with this view through thick and thin in the years ahead. So would Brzezinski, who had long subscribed to the same idea and who now advocated a speedy withdrawal from Iraq ("a manageable, though serious, challenge of largely regional origin" that "the Bush team" had turned "into an international debacle") for the express purpose of shifting our focus back to "the Israeli-Palestinian peace process."

But whether the conflict between Israel and the Palestinians was truly "the obsession of the region" or, rather, a screen for other things, it undoubtedly was the obsession of Brzezinski and Scowcroft, as it was of almost everyone else who looked at the Middle East from the so-called realist perspective and to whom stability was the great desideratum.

Yet even from that perspective, the nonstop preoccupation with Israel would only be warranted if the conflict with the Palestinians were the main cause of instability throughout the region. This was clearly what Brzezinski, Scowcroft, and most other members of the realist school believed. However, the very realities to which they were presumably so deferential made utter nonsense of this idea. Since the birth of Israel in 1948, there had been something like two dozen wars in the Middle East (variously involving Egypt, Yemen, Lebanon, Syria, Iran, and Iraq) that had had nothing whatever to do with the Jewish state or with the Palestinians. In one of these alone—the Iran-Iraq War of 1980–88—many more lives had been lost than in all the wars involving Israel put together.

The obsessive animus against Israel went hand in hand with the overall strategy for dealing with the Middle East that had prevailed before 9/11, and to which Brzezinski and Scowcroft were still married, heart and soul and mind. The best and most succinct description of that strategy had been given by President Bush himself in explaining why 9/11 had driven him to reject it in favor of a radically different approach:

> In the past . . . long-standing ties often led us to overlook the faults of local elites. Yet this bargain did not bring stability or make us safe. It merely bought time, while problems festered and ideologies of violence took hold.

According to Jeffrey Goldberg of *The New Yorker*, when George W. Bush's second secretary of state, Condoleezza Rice, to whom Scowcroft had once been a mentor, quoted these words to him, he responded that the policy Bush was rejecting had actually brought us "fifty years of peace." (What, asked James Taranto of the *Wall Street Journal*, "do you call someone" who can describe the many wars that have been fought in the Middle East in the past five decades as "fifty years of peace"? Taranto's sardonic answer: "A 'realist.' ")

In addition to remaining convinced that the old way of doing things was right, Scowcroft was utterly disdainful of the new approach being followed by George W. Bush, which aimed (in my own preferred summation) to make the Middle East safe for America by making it safe for democracy. "I believe," he declared in his answer to Condoleezza Rice, "that you cannot with one sweep of the hand or the mind cast off thousands of years of history." But here again the so-called realist ignored the reality, which was that the Middle East of today was not thousands of years old, and was not created in the seventh century by Allah or the Prophet Muhammad. Nor had the miserable despotisms there evolved through some inexorable historical process powered entirely by internal cultural forces. Instead, the states in question had all been conjured into existence less than one hundred years ago out of the ruins of the defeated Ottoman empire in World War I. Their boundaries had been drawn by the victorious British and French with the stroke of an often arbitrary pen, and their hapless peoples were handed over in due course to one tyrant after another.

This being the case, there was nothing "utopian" about the idea that such regimes—which had been planted with shallow roots by two Western powers and whose legitimacy was constantly challenged by internal forces both religious and secular—could be uprooted with the help of a third Western power and that a better political system could be put in their place. Nor was it unrealistic to wonder why it should have been taken as axiomatic that these states would and/or should last forever in their present forms, and why the political configuration of the Middle East should be eternally immune from the democratizing forces that had been sweeping other parts of the world. And in fact, though Scowcroft kept insisting that "you're not going to democratize Iraq," and certainly not "in any reasonable time frame," in the span of three short years Iraq, although still suffering from the effects of "post-totalitarian syndrome," had already taken several giant steps toward democratization.

Given the convictions in which Scowcroft had invested a lifetime of belief and practice, how could he not have rooted for an American defeat in Iraq and the discredit it would bring down upon the head of the Bush Doctrine?

And yet, while the campaign to discredit the Bush Doctrine may have been doing brilliantly in the United States, the exiled Iranian commentator Amir Taheri composed a vividly concrete account of how miserably the parallel campaign being waged by the insurgency was failing in Iraq:

> They kill teachers and children, but schools stay open. They kill doctors and patients, but hospitals still function. They kill civil servants, but the ministries are crawling back into operation. They kidnap and murder foreign businessmen, but more keep coming. They massacre volunteers for the new army and police, but the lines of those wishing to join grow longer. They blow up

pipelines and kill oil workers, but oil still flows. They kill judges and lawyers, but Iraq's new courts keep on working. They machine-gun buses carrying foreign pilgrims, but the pilgrims come back in growing numbers. They kill newspaper boys, but newspapers still get delivered every day.

Nibras Kazimi, an Iraqi writer now living in the United States, provided a similar description:

It is easy for journalists to ride the "Iraq is failing" wave and churn out the safe stories that tell us that all is bad. It is much harder for them to make sense of why so many Iraqi policemen and soldiers are fighting back when attacked rather than dropping their weapons and cowering for safety. Something is changing in Iraq, and it is happening despite the serial bungling of [Prime Minister] Maliki's government or the incessant predictions of an American withdrawal. It is happening because more and more Iraqis understand what is at stake should those murderous insurgents win.

Nevertheless, as time went on fewer and fewer Americans seemed to share in this understanding of what was at stake in Iraq, not only for the people living there but for us in the United States as well. It was an ominous development, and it would prove to have very serious consequences in the months and years ahead.

CHAPTER ELEVEN

THE RADICALIZATION
OF THE DEMOCRATS

WITH SO RELENTLESS an assault on the Bush Doctrine coming from so many quarters in the world of ideas, it was inevitable that antiwar sentiment would seep into the world of electoral politics. I have already spoken of my amazement in the months after 9/11 at how far and how fast the antiwar movement had already managed to go. But I had not yet seen the half of it. Whereas it took twelve years for the radicals I addressed in that drafty union hall in 1960 to capture the Democratic Party behind George McGovern, their political and spiritual heirs of 2001 seemed to be pulling off the same trick in less than two. This time their leader of choice was the raucously antiwar Howard Dean. Though he eventually failed to win the Democratic nomination for president in 2004, his early successes frightened most of the relatively moderate candidates into a sharp leftward turn on Iraq and drove out the few who still supported the campaign there. As for John Kerry, in order to win the nomination, he had to disavow the vote he had cast in 2002 authorizing the president to use force against Saddam Hussein.

In doing so, Kerry borrowed a tactic from the antiwar movement of the Vietnam days—a movement of which he was more truly a veteran (having after his discharge from the Navy become a leader of Vietnam Veterans Against the War) than he had been of the war itself.* But this particular maneuver was only one example of how—even though, as I said earlier, in all other respects Vietnam and Iraq had nothing whatever in common—the antiwar movement that developed in opposition to the one developed into a virtual clone of the other. In this instance, Kerry did exactly what had been done by the many congressmen and senators who in 1975 had voted for the Gulf of Tonkin resolution authorizing Lyndon Johnson to use force against North Vietnam and who had subsequently changed their minds. Like them, Kerry claimed that he had been deceived by the president.**

It did not take long for this charge of deception to move from the hustings into the halls of Congress, where it donned the camouflage of a series of allegedly nonpartisan hearings. In these hearings, the most prominent of which was the one held by the Senate Intelligence Committee, high officials of the Bush administration were hectored by the Democratic members (and even a few of the Republicans) in terms that often came close to sounding like the many articles and books already in circulation purporting to prove that George W. Bush had duped us into an immoral and/or unnecessary war in Iraq by feeding us a pack of lies that had now been exposed for all to see. It was a charge that would live on beyond the 2004 election and would survive any and all of the definitive

---

* After his discharge from the Navy he became a leader of Vietnam Veterans Against the War, and in that capacity he charged that our forces had committed innumerable war crimes there on a "day-to-day basis": "They . . . raped, cut off ears, cut off heads, taped wires from portable telephones to human genitals and turned up the power, cut off limbs, blown up [sic] bodies, randomly shot at civilians, razed villages in fashion [sic] reminiscent of Genghis Khan, shot cattle and dogs for fun, poisoned food stocks, and generally ravaged the countryside of South Vietnam." All this was based on testimony at a staged hearing in Detroit that was later largely discredited by the Naval Investigation Service, which found, among other things, that some of the "witnesses" had not even been present at the hearing and that others were either unwilling or unable to provide details of the atrocities they had claimed to have seen or committed themselves.
** Incidentally, a good case can be made that Johnson, although wrong about the Gulf of Tonkin, believed what he said about it to Congress.

refutations that should have been enough, and more than enough, to kill it off.*

The main lie that the president was accused of telling was that Saddam Hussein possessed an arsenal of weapons of mass destruction, or WMD, as they invariably came to be called. From this followed the subsidiary "lie" that Iraq under Saddam's regime had posed a two-edged mortal threat. On the one hand, the administration had allegedly declared that there was a distinct (or even an "imminent") possibility that Saddam himself would use these weapons against us and/or our allies; on the other hand, there was the still more danger-ous possibility that he would supply them to terrorists like those who had already attacked us on 9/11 and to whom he was linked.

Yet even stipulating—which I do only for the sake of argu-ment—that no weapons of mass destruction existed in Iraq in the period leading up to the invasion, it defied all reason to think that Bush was lying when he asserted that they did. To lie means to say something one knows to be false. But there could be no doubt whatsoever that Bush believed in the truth of what he was saying about WMD in Iraq.

How indeed could it have been otherwise? After all, George Tenet, his own CIA director, had assured him that the case was "a slam-dunk." This phrase would later become notorious, but in us-ing it, Tenet had had the backing of all fifteen agencies involved in gathering intelligence for the United States. In the National Intelligence Estimate (NIE) of 2002, where their collective views were summarized, one of the conclusions offered with "high con-fidence" was that

> Iraq is continuing, and in some areas expanding its chemical, bio-
> logical, nuclear, and missile programs contrary to UN resolutions.

* Shades of what Clare Boothe Luce, among other opponents of Franklin Roosevelt on the Right, said about him after Pearl Harbor: that he had "lied us into war because he didn't have the courage to lead us into it." But this charge, which would, as we have seen, be refuted by Roberta Wohlsetter, never acquired the traction of the one against Bush.

The intelligence agencies of Britain, Germany, Russia, China, Israel, and—yes—France had all agreed with this judgment. And even Hans Blix—who had headed the UN team of inspectors trying to determine whether Saddam had complied with the demands of the Security Council that he get rid of the weapons of mass destruction he was known to have used in the past against Iran and also against his own Kurdish population—lent further credibility to the case in a report issued only a few months before the invasion:

> The discovery of a number of 122-mm chemical rocket warheads in a bunker at a storage depot 170 km southwest of Baghdad was much publicized. This was a relatively new bunker, and therefore the rockets must have been moved there in the past few years, at a time when Iraq should not have had such munitions. . . . They could also be the tip of a submerged iceberg. The discovery of a few rockets does not resolve but rather points to the issue of several thousands of chemical rockets that are unaccounted for.

Blix would later claim that he was only being "cautious" here, but if, as he would then also add, the Bush administration had "misled itself" in interpreting the evidence before it, he at the very least had lent it a helping hand.

So, once again, had the British, the French, and the Germans, all of whom had signed on in advance to Secretary of State Colin Powell's reading of the satellite photos he presented to the UN in the period leading up to the invasion. Powell himself and his chief of staff, Lawrence Wilkerson, later came to feel that this speech was the low point of his tenure as secretary of state. But Wilkerson was forced to acknowledge (in the process of a vicious attack on the president, the vice president, and the secretary of defense for getting us into Iraq) that the Bush administration had not lacked for company in interpreting the available evidence as it did:

> I can't tell you why the French, the Germans, the Brits, and us thought that most of the material, if not all of it, that we pre-

sented at the UN on 5 February 2003 was the truth. I can't. I've wrestled with it. [But] when you see a satellite photograph of all the signs of the chemical-weapons ASP—Ammunition Supply Point—with chemical weapons, and you match all those signs with your matrix on what should show a chemical ASP, and they're there, you have to conclude that it's a chemical ASP, especially when you see the next satellite photograph which shows the UN inspectors wheeling in their white vehicles with black markings on them to that same ASP, and everything is changed, everything is clean. . . . But George [Tenet] was convinced, John McLaughlin [Tenet's deputy] was convinced, that what we were presented [for Powell's UN speech] was accurate.

Going on to shoot down a widespread impression, Wilkerson had revealed that even the State Department's Bureau of Intelligence and Research (INR) was convinced:

People say, well, INR dissented. That's a bunch of bull. INR dissented that the nuclear program was up and running. That's all INR dissented on. They were right there with the chems and the bios.

Thus, in explaining its dissent on Iraq's nuclear program, the INR had, as stated in the National Intelligence Estimate of 2002, expressed doubt about

Iraq's efforts to acquire aluminum tubes [which are] central to the argument that Baghdad is reconstituting its nuclear-weapons program. . . . INR is not persuaded that the tubes in question are intended for use as centrifuge rotors . . . in Iraq's nuclear-weapons program.

But, according to Wilkerson,

the French came in in the middle of my deliberations at the CIA and said, we have just spun aluminum tubes, and by God, we did it to this RPM, et cetera, et cetera, and it was all, you know, proof positive that the aluminum tubes were not for mortar casings or artillery casings, they were for centrifuges. Otherwise, why would you have such exquisite instruments?

In short—and whether or not it had included the secret heart of Hans Blix—"the consensus of the intelligence community," as Wilkerson put it, "was overwhelming" in the period leading up to the invasion of Iraq that Saddam definitely had an arsenal of chemical and biological weapons and that he was also in all probability well on the way to rebuilding the nuclear capability that the Israelis had damaged by bombing the Osirak reactor in 1981.

Additional confirmation of this latter point would come from Kenneth Pollack, who had served in the National Security Council under Clinton. "In the late spring of 2002," Pollack would write,

> I participated in a Washington meeting about Iraqi WMD. Those present included nearly twenty former inspectors from the United Nations Special Commission (UNSCOM), the force established in 1991 to oversee the elimination of WMD in Iraq. One of the senior people put a question to the group: did anyone in the room doubt that Iraq was currently operating a secret centrifuge plant? No one did. Three people added that they believed Iraq was also operating a secret calutron plant (a facility for separating uranium isotopes).

No wonder, then, that another conclusion the National Intelligence Estimate of 2002 had reached with "high confidence" was that

> Iraq could make a nuclear weapon in months to a year once it acquires sufficient weapons-grade fissile material.

But the consensus on which Bush had relied was not born in his own administration. In fact, it had first been fully formed in the Clinton administration. Here was Clinton himself, speaking in 1998:

If Saddam rejects peace and we have to use force, our purpose is clear. We want to seriously diminish the threat posed by Iraq's weapons-of-mass-destruction program.

Here was his secretary of state, Madeleine Albright, also speaking in 1998:

Iraq is a long way from [the United States], but what happens there matters a great deal here. For the risk that the leaders of a rogue state will use nuclear, chemical, or biological weapons against us or our allies is the greatest security threat we face.

Here was Sandy Berger, Clinton's national security adviser, who chimed in at the same time with this flat-out assertion about Saddam:

He will use those weapons of mass destruction again, as he has ten times since 1983.

Finally, Clinton's secretary of defense, William Cohen, was so sure Saddam had stockpiles of WMD that he remained "absolutely convinced" of it even after our failure to find them in the wake of the invasion in March 2003.

Nor did leading Democrats in Congress entertain any doubts on this score. A few months after Clinton and his people made the statements I have just quoted, a group of Democratic senators, including such liberals as Carl Levin, Tom Daschle, and John Kerry himself, urged the president

to take necessary actions (including, if appropriate, air and missile strikes on suspect Iraqi sites) to respond effectively to the threat posed by Iraq's refusal to end its weapons-of-mass-destruction programs.

Nancy Pelosi, the future leader of the Democrats in the House and at that time a member of the House Intelligence Committee, added her voice to the chorus:

Saddam Hussein has been engaged in the development of weapons-of-mass-destruction technology, which is a threat to countries in the region, and he has made a mockery of the weapons inspection process.

This Democratic drumbeat continued and even intensified when Bush succeeded Clinton in 2001, and it featured many who would later pretend to have been deceived by the Bush White House. In a letter to the new president, a number of senators, led by the Democrat Bob Graham, declared:

> There is no doubt that . . . Saddam Hussein has invigorated his weapons programs. Reports indicate that biological, chemical, and nuclear programs continue apace and may be back to pre–Gulf War status. In addition, Saddam continues to redefine delivery systems and is doubtless using the cover of a licit missile program to develop longer-range missiles that will threaten the United States and our allies.

Senator Carl Levin also reaffirmed for Bush's benefit what he had told Clinton some years earlier:

> Saddam Hussein is a tyrant and a threat to the peace and stability of the region. He has ignored the mandate of the United Nations, and is building weapons of mass destruction and the means of delivering them.

Senator Hillary Rodham Clinton agreed, speaking in October 2002:

> In the four years since the inspectors left, intelligence reports show that Saddam Hussein has worked to rebuild his chemical- and biological-weapons stock, his missile-delivery capability, and his nuclear program. He has also given aid, comfort, and sanctuary to terrorists, including Al Qaeda members.

Senator Jay Rockefeller, vice chairman of the Senate Intelligence Committee (who would later loudly proclaim that he had been deceived by Bush), agreed as well:

> There is unmistakable evidence that Saddam Hussein is working aggressively to develop nuclear weapons and will likely have nuclear weapons within the next five years. . . . We also should remember we have always underestimated the progress Saddam has made in development of weapons of mass destruction.

And Harry Reid, the future Democratic leader in the Senate who in that position would also claim to have been deceived and would denounce the invasion of Iraq as "the worst foreign-policy mistake" in American history, subscribed to the opposite view in 2002:

> Saddam Hussein in effect has thumbed his nose at the world community, and I think that the president is approaching this in the right fashion.

Even more striking were the sentiments of Bush's opponents in his two campaigns for the presidency. Thus, Al Gore in September 2002:

> We know that [Saddam] has stored secret supplies of biological and chemical weapons throughout his country.

And here was Gore again, in that same year:

> Iraq's search for weapons of mass destruction has proven impossible to deter, and we should assume that it will continue for as long as Saddam is in power.

Now to John Kerry, also speaking in 2002:

> I will be voting to give the president of the United States the authority to use force—if necessary—to disarm Saddam Hussein

because I believe that a deadly arsenal of weapons of mass destruction in his hands is a real and grave threat to our security.

Perhaps most startling of all, given the vituperative rhetoric they would later employ against Bush after the invasion of Iraq, were statements made by Senators Ted Kennedy and Robert Byrd, also in 2002:

> *Kennedy:* We have known for many years that Saddam Hussein is seeking and developing weapons of mass destruction.
> *Byrd:* The last UN weapons inspectors left Iraq in October of 1998. We are confident that Saddam Hussein retains some stockpiles of chemical and biological weapons, and that he has since embarked on a crash course to build up his chemical- and biological-warfare capabilities. Intelligence reports indicate that he is seeking nuclear weapons.

Liberal politicians like these were seconded by the mainstream media, in whose columns a very different tune would also later be sung. For example, throughout the last two years of the Clinton administration, editorials in the *New York Times* repeatedly insisted that

> without further outside intervention, Iraq should be able to rebuild weapons and missile plants within a year [and] future military attacks may be required to diminish the arsenal again.

The *Times* was also skeptical of negotiations, pointing out that it was

> hard to negotiate with a tyrant who has no intention of honoring his commitments and who sees nuclear, chemical, and biological weapons as his country's salvation.

So, too, the *Washington Post*, which greeted the inauguration of George W. Bush in January 2001 with the admonition that of all the booby traps left behind by the Clinton administration, none is more dangerous—or more urgent—than the situation in Iraq. Over the last year, Mr. Clinton and his team quietly avoided dealing with, or calling attention to, the almost complete unraveling of a decade's efforts to isolate the regime of Saddam Hussein and prevent it from rebuilding its weapons of mass destruction. That leaves President Bush to confront a dismaying panorama in the Persian Gulf [where] intelligence photos . . . show the reconstruction of factories long suspected of producing chemical and biological weapons.*

All this should have sufficed to prove far beyond any even unreasonable doubt that Bush had been telling what he believed to be the truth about Saddam's stockpile of WMD. It also disposed of the fallback charge that Bush had lied by exaggerating or "hyping" or "cherry-picking" the intelligence presented to him.

Even so, this charge was given a certain amount of credence by the leak of the so-called Downing Street memo describing a meeting of the British Cabinet on July 23, 2002. The key passage read as follows:

C [the head of MI6, the British counterpart to the CIA] reported on his recent talks in Washington. . . . Military action was now seen as inevitable. Bush wanted to remove Saddam, through military action, justified by the conjunction of terrorism and WMD. But the intelligence and facts were being fixed around the policy.

Yet even leaving aside the fact that the word *fixed* in British usage means "organized around" rather than "faked," it is clear from the six other memos that also came to light at the same time that they do not prove, as gleefully charged by opponents of the war, that

---

* I am reminded of the story the blogger James Lileks tells about confronting a Democratic Bush-hater with the evidence that everyone in the Clinton administration believed that Saddam had WMD. "Maybe so," came the reply, "but at least they never *did* anything about it."

Bush was lying about the WMD. As Fred Kaplan of *Slate*, no friend (to put it mildly) of Bush or of the invasion of Iraq, sums up what the seven memos "quite clearly" reveal about the "top leaders in the U.S. and British governments":

> These top officials genuinely believed that Iraq had weapons of mass destruction—and that they constituted a threat. They believed that the international community had to be sold on the matter. But not all sales pitches are consciously deceptive. The salesmen in this case turned out to be *wrong*; their goods were bunk. But they seemed to believe in their product at the time.

Indeed, why on earth should they not have believed "in their product" when the intelligence itself was so compelling that it convinced everyone who had direct access to it, and when hardly anyone in the world thought that Saddam had, as he claimed, complied with the sixteen resolutions of the Security Council demanding that he get rid of his weapons of mass destruction?

Hillary Clinton, who never demurred from the "Bush lied" mantra when it was serving her party's political interests, would later admit to an interviewer that she had thought even then that Bush

> believed, as I believed, that there was, at the very least, residual weapons of mass destruction, and whether the Iraqis ever intended to let the inspectors go forward was being answered year by year. There was a lot of evidence that this was not their intention.

Even more telling would be the belated admission by Senator John Edwards, who as John Kerry's running mate in 2004 had silently acquiesced in the excuse that Bush's lies about weapons of mass destruction had misled him and others, that the lie was on the other foot:

I was convinced that Saddam had chemical and biological weapons and was doing everything in his power to get nuclear weapons. . . . I didn't rely on George Bush for that. And I personally think there's some dishonesty in suggesting that members of the United States Senate relied on George Bush for that information, because I don't think it's true. It's great politics. But it's not the truth. . . . I've just heard people say, "Well, you know, George Bush . . . misled us." . . . I was there, it's not what happened. . . . I was on the Intelligence Committee, so I got direct information from the intelligence community. And then I had a series of meetings with former Clinton administration people. And they were all saying the same thing. Everything I was hearing in the Intelligence Committee was the same thing I was hearing from these guys. And there was nary a dissenting voice.

Another fallback charge was that Bush, operating mainly through Cheney, had somehow forced the CIA into telling him what he wanted to hear. Yet in its report of 2004, the bipartisan Senate Intelligence Committee, while criticizing the CIA for relying on what in hindsight looked like weak or faulty intelligence, stated that it

did not find any evidence that administration officials attempted to coerce, influence, or pressure analysts to change their judgments related to Iraq's weapons-of-mass-destruction capabilities.

The March 2005 report of the equally bipartisan Robb-Silberman Commission, set up to investigate intelligence failures on Iraq, reached the same conclusion, finding

no evidence of political pressure to influence the intelligence community's pre-war assessments of Iraq's weapons programs. . . . Analysts universally asserted that in no instance did political pressure cause them to skew or alter any of their analytical judgments.

Still, even many who had believed that Saddam possessed WMD, and was ruthless enough to use them, accused Bush of telling a different sort of lie by characterizing the risk as "imminent." But this, too, was false. Although Senator John Edwards, later to become Kerry's running mate in 2004, and Jay Rockefeller, the ranking Democrat on the Senate Intelligence Committee, actually did use the word *imminence* in describing the threat posed by Saddam, Bush consistently *rejected* imminence as a justification for war. Thus, in the State of the Union address he delivered only three months after 9/11, Bush declared that he would "not wait on events while dangers gather" and that he would "not stand by, as peril draws closer and closer." Then, in his speech at West Point six months later, he reiterated the same point: "If we wait for threats to materialize, we will have waited too long." And as if that were not clear enough, he went out of his way in his State of the Union address in 2003 (that is, three months before the invasion), to bring up the word *imminent* itself precisely in order to repudiate it:

> Some have said we must not act until the threat is imminent. Since when have terrorists and tyrants announced their intentions, politely putting us on notice before they strike? If this threat is permitted to fully and suddenly emerge, all actions, all words, and all recriminations would come too late. Trusting in the sanity and restraint of Saddam Hussein is not a strategy, and it is not an option.

What of the related charge that it was still another lie to suggest, as Bush and his people had, that a connection could be traced between Saddam Hussein and the Al Qaeda terrorists who had attacked us on 9/11? This charge would also be rejected by the Senate Intelligence Committee. Contrary to how its findings would be summarized in the mainstream media, the committee's report would explicitly conclude that Al Qaeda had in fact had a cooperative, if informal, relationship with Iraqi agents working under Saddam. The report of the bipartisan 9/11 Commission would come to the same conclusion, as would a comparably independent British investigation conducted by Lord Butler, which would point to "meetings . . . between senior Iraqi representatives and senior al-Qaeda operatives."

If, given all this, George W. Bush had failed to take action against Iraq, he would have been guilty of an egregious dereliction of his responsibility to "preserve, protect, and defend" this country "against all enemies, foreign and domestic," and for that he would truly have deserved to be impeached.

Turning now, finally, to what in my judgment was the most disgraceful instance of all in this lengthy catalog of lying charges against George W. Bush for lying, there was the story of Joseph C. Wilson IV.

The story began with the notorious sixteen words inserted—after, be it noted, much vetting by the CIA and the State Department—into Bush's 2003 State of the Union address:

> The British government has learned that Saddam Hussein recently sought significant quantities of uranium from Africa.

This was the "lie" Wilson bragged of having "debunked" after being sent by the CIA to Niger in 2002 to check out the intelligence it had received to that effect (". . . if the president had been referring to Niger, then his conclusion was not borne out by the facts as I understood them.")

Wilson would later angrily deny that his wife, Valerie Plame, who worked in some unknown capacity at the CIA, had recommended him for this mission, and he would do his best to spread the impression that choosing him had been the vice president's idea. He would also later charge that someone in the Bush administration, and probably on Cheney's staff, had broken the law by "outing" his wife's name. The supposed purpose of leaking this supposedly classified information to the press had been to retaliate against Wilson for having "debunked" (in his words) "the lies that

led to war," and it had led to the appointment of a special prose-
cutor named Patrick Fitzgerald who would spend more than two
years ostensibly searching for the leaker.*

As to whether Cheney had recommended him for the mission,
this turned out to be only one of Wilson's many lies. Even Nicholas
Kristof of the *New York Times*, through whom Wilson first planted
this impression, was eventually forced to admit that "Cheney apparently didn't know that Wilson had been dispatched." (By the
time Kristof grudgingly issued this retraction, Wilson himself, in
characteristically shameless fashion, was denying that he had ever
"said the vice president sent me or ordered me sent.") And as for his
wife's supposed nonrole in his mission, here was what Valerie
Plame Wilson wrote in a memo to her boss at the CIA:

> My husband has good relations with the PM [the prime minister
> of Niger] and the former minister of mines . . . both of whom
> could possibly shed light on this sort of activity.

More than a year after his return, with the help of Kristof and
also Walter Pincus of the *Washington Post*, and then through an
op-ed piece in the *Times* under his own name, Wilson succeeded, probably beyond his wildest dreams, in setting off a political firestorm.

In response, the White House, no doubt hoping to prevent his
allegation about the sixteen words from becoming a proxy for the
charge that (in one of Wilson's many iterations of it) "lies and dis-
information [were] used to justify the invasion of Iraq," eventually
acknowledged that the president's statement "did not rise to the
level of inclusion in the State of the Union address." As the White
House should have anticipated, however, this panicky response
served to make things worse rather than better. And yet it was to-

---

* "Ostensibly" because it would eventually be revealed that the leaker had been
Richard Armitage of the State Department and that Fitzgerald had discovered
this very early in his investigation. Yet even though this alone proved that the
leak had not come from the White House as part of a conspiracy to harm Wilson
and his wife, Fitzgerald went doggedly on.

tally unnecessary—for the maddeningly simple reason that every single one of the sixteen words at issue was *true*.

That is, British intelligence *had* assured the CIA that Saddam Hussein had tried to buy enriched uranium from the African country of Niger. Furthermore—and notwithstanding the endlessly repeated assertion that this assurance had later been discredited—Britain's independent Butler Commission concluded that it was "well founded." The relevant passage is worth quoting at length:

a. It is accepted by all parties that Iraqi officials visited Niger in 1999.
b. The British government had intelligence from several different sources indicating that this visit was for the purpose of acquiring uranium. Since uranium constitutes almost three-quarters of Niger's exports, the intelligence was credible.
c. The evidence was not conclusive that Iraq actually purchased, as opposed to having sought, uranium, and the British government did not claim this.

As if that were not enough to settle the matter, Wilson himself, far from challenging the British report when he was "debriefed" on his return from Niger (although challenging it was what he would never stop doing in the future), had actually strengthened the CIA's belief in its accuracy. From the Senate Intelligence Committee report:

He [the CIA reports officer] said he judged that the most important fact in the report [by Wilson] was that Niger officials admitted that the Iraqi delegation had traveled there in 1999, and that the Niger prime minister believed the Iraqis were interested in purchasing uranium.

And again:

The report on [Wilson's] trip to Niger . . . did not change any analysts' assessments of the Iraq-Niger uranium deal. For most analysts, the information in the report lent more credibility to the original CIA reports on the uranium deal.

This passage went on to note that the State Department's Bureau of Intelligence and Research—which (as we have already seen) did not believe that Saddam Hussein was trying to develop nuclear weapons—found support in Wilson's report for its "assessment that Niger was unlikely to be willing or able to sell uranium to Iraq." But if so, this, as the Butler report quoted here pointed out, would not mean that Iraq had not *tried* to buy it—which was the only claim made by British intelligence and then by Bush in the famous sixteen words.

The liar here, then, was not Bush but Wilson. And Wilson also lied when he told the *Washington Post* that he had unmasked as forgeries certain documents given to American intelligence (forged by whom it has never become clear) that supposedly contained additional evidence of Saddam's efforts to buy uranium from Niger. The documents did indeed turn out to be forgeries, but, according to the Butler report,

> the forged documents were not available to the British government at the time its assessment was made, and so the fact of the forgery does not undermine [that assessment].

More damning yet to Wilson, the Senate Intelligence Committee discovered that he had never laid eyes on the documents in question:

> [Wilson] also told committee staff that he was the source of a *Washington Post* article . . . which said, "Among the envoy's conclusions was that the documents may have been forged because 'the dates were wrong and the names were wrong.' " Committee staff asked how the former ambassador could have come to the conclusion that the "dates were wrong and the names were wrong" when he had never seen the CIA reports and had no knowledge of what names and dates were in the reports.

To top all this off, just as Cheney had had nothing to do with the choice of Wilson for the mission to Niger, neither was it true that, as Wilson "confirmed" for a credulous *New Republic* reporter, "the CIA circulated [his] report to the vice president's office," thereby supposedly proving that Cheney and his staff "knew the Niger story was a flat-out lie." Yet—the mind reels—if Cheney had actually been briefed on Wilson's oral report to the CIA (which he never was), he would, like the CIA itself, have been *more* inclined to believe that Saddam had tried to buy yellowcake uranium from Niger.

So much for the author of the best-selling and much acclaimed book whose title alone—*The Politics of Truth: Inside the Lies That Led to War and Betrayed My Wife's CIA Identity*—set new records both for chutzpah and for mendacity.

In the wake of the WMD issue, several others emerged that gave new heart to the opponents of the operation in Iraq. On top of the mounting number of American soldiers being killed as they were trying to bring security to Iraq, and on the heels of such horrendous episodes as the murder and desecration of the bodies of four American contractors in Falluja, came the revelation that Iraqi prisoners in Abu Ghraib had been subjected to ugly mistreatment by their American captors.

That the antiwar movement would harp on all this—and would continue ignoring the enormous progress we had made in the reconstruction of Iraqi society—was only to be expected. It was also only natural for the Democrats to take as much political advantage of the setbacks as they could. But it was not necessarily to be expected that the Democrats would seize just as eagerly as the radicals upon every piece of bad news as another weapon in the war against the war. Still less was it to be expected that mainstream Democratic politicians would go so far off the intellectual and moral rails as to compare the harassment and humiliation of the prisoners in Abu Ghraib—none of whom, so far as anyone knew, was even maimed, let alone killed—to the horrendous torturing and murdering that had gone on in that same prison under

Saddam Hussein or, even more outlandishly, to the Soviet gulag in which many millions of prisoners died.

Yet this was what Edward M. Kennedy did on the floor of the Senate, where he declared that the torture chamber of Saddam Hussein had been reopened "under new management—U.S. management," and this was what Al Gore did when he accused Bush of "establishing an American gulag." Joining with the politicians was the main financial backer of the Democratic Party's presidential campaign, George Soros, who actually said that Abu Ghraib was even worse than the attack of 9/11. On the platform with Soros when he made this morally disgusting statement was Senator Hillary Rodham Clinton, who let it go by without a peep of protest.

Equally ignominious was the response of mainstream Democrats to the most effective demagogic exfoliation of the antiwar radicals, Michael Moore's film *Fahrenheit 9/11*. Shortly after 9/11—that is, long before the appearance of this movie but with many of its charges against Bush already on vivid display in Moore's public statements about Afghanistan—one liberal commentator had described him as a "well-known crank, regarded with considerable distaste even on the Left." The same commentator (shades of how the "jackal bins" of yore were regarded) had also dismissed as "preposterous" the idea that Moore's views "represent a significant body of antiwar opinion." Lending a measure of plausibility to this assessment was the fact that Moore had elicited a few boos when, in accepting an Academy Award for *Bowling for Columbine* in 2003, he had declared:

> We live in the time where we have fictitious election results that elect a fictitious president. We live in a time where we have a man sending us to war for fictitious reasons. . . . We are against this war, Mr. Bush. Shame on you, Mr. Bush, shame on you.

By 2004, however, when *Fahrenheit 9/11* came out, things had changed. True, this movie—a compendium of every scurrility ever hurled at George W. Bush and a few new ones besides, all gleefully stitched together in the best conspiratorial tradition of the "paranoid style in American politics" that had once been associated entirely with the Right—did manage to embarrass even several liberal commentators. One of them described the film as a product of the "loony Left" and feared that its extremism might discredit the "legitimate" case against Bush and the war. Yet in an amazing reversal of the normal pattern in the distribution of prudence, such fears of extremism were more pronounced among liberal pundits than among mainstream Democratic politicians.

Thus, so many leading Democrats flocked to a screening of *Fahrenheit 9/11* in Washington that (as the columnist Mark Steyn quipped) the business of Congress had to be put on hold, and when the screening was over, nary a dissonant boo disturbed the harmony of the ensuing ovation. The then chairman of the Democratic National Committee, Terry McAuliffe, pronounced the film "very powerful, much more powerful than I thought it would be." Then, when asked by CNN whether he thought "the movie was essentially fair and factually based," McAuliffe answered, "I do. . . . Clearly the movie makes it clear that George Bush is not fit to be president of this country." Senator Tom Harkin of Iowa seconded McAuliffe and urged all Americans to see the film:

> It's important for the American people to understand what has gone on before, what led us to this point, and to see it sort of in this unvarnished presentation by Michael Moore.

Possibly some of the other important Democrats who attended the screening—including Senators Tom Daschle, Max Baucus, Barbara Boxer, and Bill Nelson; Congressmen Charles Rangel, Henry Waxman, and Jim McDermott; and elders of the party like Arthur Schlesinger Jr. and Theodore Sorensen—disagreed with Harkin and McAuliffe. But if so, they remained remarkably quiet about it. As for John Kerry himself, he did not take time out to see *Fahrenheit 9/11*, explaining that there was no need to do so since he had "lived it."

A few months later, Moore was seated in no less a place of honor at the Democratic National Convention than the box of Jimmy Carter. Yet the convention itself did not reflect the antiwar attitudes he represented. On accepting the nomination, Kerry presented himself not as a leader of Vietnam Veterans Against the War but as a proud veteran of that war. He saluted, announced that he was "reporting for duty," and surrounded himself with a crowd of the men who had served with him. Because of this display of hawkishness, it seemed possible that if he were to win, the Democratic Party might sober up and dissociate itself from radicals like Moore. Conceivably this might have happened, but another defeat only served, if anything, to deepen the Democrats' bitterness and intensify their rage against George W. Bush, and especially over Iraq.

At first, to be sure, the attacks they continued to mount were largely aimed at the "incompetence" with which the war was being fought, but before long they were just as feverish as the radicals in trying to delegitimize it altogether. Having failed during the presidential campaign to persuade enough voters that the Bush administration had lied us into the war, they returned to the charge with redoubled energy after the election was over. Leaning heavily on a turn in public opinion that had largely been brought about by the harping of the mainstream media on how badly things were going in Iraq, the Democrats inched closer and closer to the position of the radicals and became less and less cautious about calling for a withdrawal of American forces from Iraq.

A goodly number of these Democrats (Howard Dean, now the chairman of the Democratic National Committee, and Congresswoman Cynthia McKinney, to name only two) had from the very beginning stood openly and unambiguously against the invasion of Iraq. But a much larger number in their heart of hearts had evidently felt the same way, and it was only the fear of being punished at the polls at a time when public support for Bush's policy was high that had made them bite their tongues. Now, however, with the polls moving in the other direction, they felt free to come out of the antiwar closet. (No wonder the radicals greeted their poll-driven change of position with contempt.)

Added to these were a certain number of Democrats who corresponded to what Tom Paine (at an equally dark moment of our own war of independence) called "the summer soldiers and the sunshine patriots." The most prominent of them was Congressman John Murtha of Pennsylvania, a former Marine who had backed the invasion of Iraq because (to give him the benefit of the doubt) he really thought it was the right thing to do, but who had now bought entirely into the view that all was lost and that the only sensible course was to turn tail:

> The war in Iraq is . . . a flawed policy wrapped in illusion. . . . Our military is suffering. The future of our country is at risk. We cannot continue on the present course. It is evident that continued military action is not in the best interests of the United States of America, the Iraqi people, or the Persian Gulf region. . . . Our troops have become the primary target of the insurgency. They are united against U.S. forces and we have become a catalyst for violence. U.S. troops are the common enemy of the Sunnis, Saddamists, and foreign jihadists. . . . Our military has done everything that has been asked of them, the U.S. cannot accomplish anything further in Iraq militarily. It is time to bring them home.

In spite of the fact that talk of this kind could only confuse and demoralize the troops for whose welfare, and for whose sufferings, Murtha expressed such concern, and in spite of the fact that it could only give new heart to the Islamofascist terrorists, Murtha's speech was greeted with a standing ovation from his fellow Democrats. A point had been reached where the only questions at issue among the Democrats were how quickly to bug out of Iraq and whether to fix a timetable and a deadline for doing so.

CHAPTER TWELVE

DEFEATISM ON THE RIGHT

A s THE DEMOCRATIC trumpet was sounding a retreat barely distinguishable from a call for surrender, a spirit of defeatism was spreading within the conservative community, where support had always been strongest for the Bush Doctrine in general and its application to Iraq in particular.

To be sure, there were conservatives who, while having little or nothing in common with the Buchananite isolationists, had for reasons of their own never been happy with George W. Bush or his doctrine. The least happy and the most outspoken was the group I once labeled (much to its annoyance) the Superhawks. Of these, the most prolific was Angelo M. Codevilla, who, in a series of essays in the *Claremont Review of Books*, accused the Bush administration of "eschewing victory" by shying away from "energetic policies that might actually produce" it, and who made no bones about his belief very early on that we would lose the war as a result. In the same vein, and in the same magazine, the novelist and political commentator Mark Helprin wrote that Bush had failed

adequately to prepare for war, to declare war, rigorously to define the enemy, to decide upon disciplines and intelligent war aims, to subjugate the economy to the common defense, or even to endorse the most elemental responsibilities of government.

In then piling a commensurate heap of scorn on the idea of transforming "the entire Islamic world into a group of peaceful democratic states" (Helprin), these two eloquent and fiery polemicists were joined by the more temperate Charles R. Kesler, the editor of the *Claremont Review*. If, said Kesler, democratization was to succeed in the regimes of the Islamic world, a necessary precondition was to do unto them what we had done unto Germany and Japan in World War II: beat them into "complete submission" and then occupy them "for decades—not just for months or years, but for decades." Even then, added Codevilla, our troops might have to "stay and die . . . indefinitely on behalf of a mission . . . concerning the accomplishment of which there is little knowledge and less agreement."

Many conservatives would undoubtedly have been tempted to line up behind this group's prescription for victory if not for its refusal to take account of the character of the American nation (even though, ironically, Codevilla himself had written a book entitled *The Character of Nations*). To the extent that the superhawks did, it was only its imperfections and deficiencies they noticed, and these—along with the constraints imposed on an American president precisely by our character, both as a nation and as a people— they waved off with derisive language, as when Codevilla referred sarcastically to "the lowest common denominator among domestic American political forces."

On the other hand, many conservatives did share their skepticism about the chances of democratizing the Middle East. Few went as far as Codevilla, who denied that we had any "right . . . to change foreign societies," but the two most important and best-known figures within the traditionalist conservative community, William F. Buckley Jr. and George Will, had entertained serious doubts from the beginning about the compatibility of the democratizing plank of the Bush Doctrine with the conservative disposition to respect and act upon the limitations of power. It took a while, however, before either of them was willing to come right out and join the opposition.

Buckley went first. In his case, the precipitating factor was the conclusion he had reached that Iraq was a lost cause. In reaching this conclusion, Buckley became part of a growing consensus. But I for one was puzzled by the amazing spread of the idea that the Bush Doctrine had already failed its first great test in Iraq. After all, Iraq had been liberated from one of the worst tyrants in the Middle East; three elections had been held; a decent constitution had been writtn; a government was in place; and previously unimaginable liberties were being enjoyed. By what bizarre calculus did all this add up to failure? And by what even stranger logic was failure to be read into the fact that the forces opposed to democratization were fighting back with all their might?

Only yesterday we had been given vivid evidence of the aspiration of most Iraqis for democratization when they flocked in their millions to the polls, and all the world had marveled at the sight. Now, because the enemies of these aspirations within Iraq and their foreign supporters were mounting a last-ditch campaign to blow them to simthereens, we were being told that it was useless to go on giving our support to what was already a failed enterprise.

To me what made more sense was the opposite interpretation of the terrible violence that was being perpetrated by the terrorists of the so-called "insurgency" and the sectarian death squads: that it was in itself a tribute to the enormous strides that had been made in democratizing and unifying the country under a workable federal system. If the sectarian militias thought that unification was a pipe dream, would they be shedding so much blood in the hope of triggering a large-scale civil war? If the murderous collection of die-hard Sunni Baathists, together with their allies inside the government, agreed that democratization had already failed, would they have been waging so desperate a campaign to defeat it? And if democratization in Iraq posed no threat to the other despotisms in the region, would they have bothered sending jihadists and material support to the "insurgency" there?

Harry V. Jaffa, another eminent conservative who (although an admirer of Bush on other grounds) thought that "the idea of bringing democracy to Iraq, or any country like Iraq, is simply utopian," had an answer to this question: they were fighting not against democratization but against each other. Yet no less an authority than the head of Al Qaeda in Iraq had once defined the nature of its struggle as, precisely, "a bitter war against the principle of democracy and all those who seek to enact it," and it was in pursuit of this objective that sectarian strife had to be provoked and exacerbated. In other words, it was impossible to distinguish between democratization and the aim of keeping the country unified, which meant that sectarian violence served the purpose not only of revenge but also of frustrating any further progress toward the loose federation envisaged by the constitution that had been adopted in a referendum the year before. Indeed, as the commentator (and retired colonel) Austin Bay would later point out:

> We know from documents captured in February 2004 that Al-Qaida saw a Sunni-Shia war as its only path to victory in Iraq. Saddam's supporters gambled that they could murder their way back into power by killing Iraqis and inciting ethnic as well as religious conflict.

Amir Taheri had a similar take on the situation:

> What is happening in Iraq . . . is neither a civil nor a sectarian war (although elements of both exist within the broader context). This war is a *political* one—between those who wish Iraq to succeed as a new democracy and those who want it to fail. Those who want the new Iraq to succeed represent the overwhelming majority of Iraqis of all ethnic and religious backgrounds. Those who want it to fail are made up of Saddamite bitter-enders, some misguided pan-Arab nationalists, death squads financed by Tehran—and a variety of non-Iraqi terrorist outfits who have come to Iraq to kill and die in the name of their perverted vision of Islam.

But returning to Buckley, in writing off Iraq, he did not immediately give up on the Bush Doctrine as a whole. For a time his position seemed to be that declaring defeat in Iraq and pulling out might be a better way to keep the doctrine alive than allowing it to die a slow death in the streets of Baghdad. But eventually, and after much hesitation, the, to him, unfortunate and definitely unconservative "ideological certitudes" of the Bush Doctrine and the evangelism of its "universalist aims" got the better of his wish to maintain solidarity with those of his political allies who were still on board. And so (possibly for the additional reason that he had come to believe that he had been wrong in sticking with Vietnam to the bitter end and did not wish to make the same mistake again) he jumped ship.

George Will waited a bit longer before joining Buckley on the newly launched conservative lifeboat. But after many months of expressing his displeasure with the Bush Doctrine, mostly through hints and suggestions, and with the fifth anniversary of 9/11 fast approaching, Will's exasperation finally boiled over. He began by lamenting that the Bush administration was "learning a lesson—one that conservatives should not have to learn on the job—about the limits of power to subdue an unruly world." This was quickly followed by an angry challenge to the idea that democratization was an antidote to terrorism. And to show just how angry he really was, he even cast a retroactive vote for John Kerry, declaring that what Kerry had once said about the war on terror— that it was "primarily an intelligence and law enforcement operation"—had now been "validated."

Will, however, did not explain why, if this approach was valid, it had failed to prevent 9/11, or why we could trust it to save us from being undone by one more such validation. Nor did he face up to an all-important fact about the Middle East of today. Like Brent Scowcroft in his quarrel with Condoleezza Rice over democratization, Will seemed to think that everything about the greater Middle East was so ancient and so deeply rooted that it would naturally repel any effort to change it. But (to repeat what I said earlier in answer to Scowcroft) the Middle East as we now knew it had been created not by Allah in the seventh century but by

British and French diplomats after World War I out of the rubble of the defeated Ottoman empire. Since these arrangements were less than a century old, there was nothing unrealistic about trying to change them. Nor, I would add in response to Will, was there anything unconservative in an effort to reshape so historically young, and so arbitrary, a political configuration.

But, against Buckley, I would also argue in more general terms that, from an indigenously American point of view, there was nothing in the least unconservative about the "ideological certitudes" and the universalism of the Bush Doctrine. For one thing, they followed closely in the tradition formed by the declared aims of the presidents who led us into the three world wars that preceded the one into which George W. Bush was leading us. The most obvious example was Woodrow Wilson, who promised to "make the world safe for democracy" by sending Americans to fight in World War I. True, the horrors and then the disillusioning aftermath of that war helped to discredit Wilson's slogan. But that did not prevent Franklin D. Roosevelt from going even further in preparing the nation for an eventual entry into World War II:

> We look forward to a world founded upon four essential human freedoms.
>
> The first is freedom of speech and expression—everywhere in the world.
>
> The second is freedom of every person to worship God in his own way—everywhere in the world.
>
> The third is freedom from want . . . —everywhere in the world.
>
> The fourth is freedom from fear . . . —anywhere in the world.

Then came Roosevelt's successor, Harry Truman. In making his appeal to Congress for aid to Greece and Turkey—both of which, he said, were threatened by Soviet-led "movements that seek to impose upon them totalitarian regimes"—Truman added that he was "fully aware of the broad implications involved," and he then went on to spell these out:

At the present moment in world history nearly every nation must choose between alternative ways of life. The choice is too often not a free one. Our way of life is based upon the will of the majority, and is distinguished by free institutions, representative government, free elections, guarantees of individual freedom, freedom of speech and religion, and freedom from political oppression. The second way of life is based upon the will of a minority forcibly imposed upon the majority. It relies upon terror and oppression, a controlled press and radio, fixed elections, and the suppression of personal freedoms.

Fourteen years later, on January 20, 1961, John F. Kennedy used religiously based universalist language strikingly similar to Bush's:

I have sworn before you and Almighty God the same solemn oath our forebears prescribed nearly a century and three quarters ago. The world is very different now. . . . And yet the same revolutionary beliefs for which our forebears fought are still at issue around the globe—the belief that the rights of man come not from the generosity of the state, but from the hand of God.

Of course, Wilson, Roosevelt, Truman, and Kennedy were all Democrats, and this fact alone might have been taken by George Will and other conservative critics of the Bush Doctrine as proof that it rested on liberal rather than conservative foundations. Indeed, many of these critics even rejected the contention often advanced by Bush and others, myself included, that the Bush Doctrine was built on the legacy of Ronald Reagan. Yet here was Reagan, speaking at Westminster Abbey on June 8, 1982:

We must be staunch in our conviction that freedom is not the sole prerogative of a lucky few, but the inalienable and universal right of all human beings. . . . It would be cultural condescension, or worse, to say that any people prefer dictatorship to democracy.

Above even Reagan, however, it was Abraham Lincoln—the greatest Republican of them all, and the greatest of all American presidents—whose spirit hovered most brightly over the face of the Bush Doctrine's universalist assumptions. Witness the following statements made by Lincoln (to which many more could easily be added):

> Those who deny freedom to others deserve it not for themselves; and, under the rule of a just God, cannot long retain it.

And again, in identifying the main principle at issue in his debates with Stephen Douglas:

> It is the eternal struggle between these two principles—right and wrong—throughout the world. They are the two principles that have stood face to face from the beginning of time; and will ever continue to struggle. . . . No matter in what shape it comes, whether from the mouth of a king who seeks to bestride the people of his own nation and live by the fruit of their labor, or from one race of men as an apology for enslaving another race, it is the same tyrannical principle.

But the universalism of the Bush Doctrine was also conservative in being rooted deep in the soil of the American political tradition. Thus, in maintaining that slavery was wrong, Lincoln appealed over the head of the Constitution (by which slavery was permitted) to the Declaration of Independence (by which it was logically forbidden):

> I believe the declaration that "all men are created equal" is the great fundamental principle upon which our free institutions rest.

To which he added:

> I should like to know if taking this old Declaration of Independence, which declares that all men are equal upon princi-

ple, and making exceptions to it, where will it stop? If one man says it does not mean a negro, why not another say it does not mean some other man?

Following in these footsteps, Bush similarly based what he called "our deepest beliefs" as Americans on the Declaration, where it was further asserted of "all men" that "they are endowed by their Creator with certain inalienable rights." As Bush put it in his Second Inaugural:

From the day of our Founding, we have proclaimed that every man and woman on this earth has rights, and dignity, and match-less value, because they bear the image of the Maker of Heaven and earth. . . . When the Declaration of Independence was first read in public and the Liberty Bell was sounded in celebration, a witness said: "It rang as if it meant something." In our time it means something still. America, in this young century, proclaims liberty throughout all the world, and to all the inhabitants thereof.

Furthermore, given the relentless attacks by Democrats on the Bush Doctrine, it is worth pointing out that the rhetoric of this president's three Democratic predecessors was if anything much more far-reaching in its universalism than his own. Roosevelt as-serted that to all human beings "everywhere in the world" no fewer than four freedoms were "essential" (even, remarkably, free-dom from fear), whereas Bush spoke only of freedom from politi-cal and religious tyranny; and while Roosevelt thought he could deliver all four of these freedoms not in "a distant millennium" but "in our own time and generation," Bush recognized that "the great objective of ending tyranny is the concentrated work of gen-erations." Admittedly Truman was a bit less sweeping than Roosevelt had been before him; he did not add "everywhere" to the "free peoples" it would be his policy to support. Still, in mov-ing from Greece and Turkey to "nearly every nation" in the world, he was sweeping enough to alarm Hans J. Morgenthau, then the leading theorist of realpolitik in the academic world, who denounced Truman for having transformed

> a concrete interest of the United States in a geographically defined part of the world into a moral principle of worldwide validity.

And if Bush never went as far as Roosevelt, and no further than Truman, he was much more restrained than Kennedy. Certainly there was nothing in any of Bush's statements to match the overkill of the most famous words Kennedy was ever to utter:

> Let every nation know, whether it wishes us well or ill, that we shall pay any price, bear any burden, meet any hardship, support any friend, oppose any foe, to assure the survival and the success of liberty.

Be all that as it may, however, it was not only traditionalist conservatives like Buckley and Will who turned for one reason or another against the Bush Doctrine. More damagingly, defections also began taking place even among the neoconservatives. The first to make his disillusionment loudly known was Francis Fukuyama, who had been a strong supporter of both the principles of the Bush Doctrine and the policies flowing from it.

Because Fukuyama was one of the most famous of the neoconservative intellectuals, and because his most famous article, "The End of History?," had supplied one of the Bush Doctrine's theoretical props, his defection was seized upon by the opposition as a happy augury of an impending neocon collapse. However, anyone who had paid close attention already knew that Fukuyama had long been harboring serious reservations about the Bush Doctrine. At first he said that it was basically sound and needed only a "recalibration," but from this mild criticism grew the conviction that, after three years of being tested in Iraq, the Bush Doctrine was now in "shambles." This also led him to a wholesale renunciation of neoconservatism ("I have concluded that neoconservatism both as a political symbol and a body of thought has evolved into something that I can no longer support"). In its place he proposed a "realistic Wilsonianism" that, give or take a detail or two, and except for its absence of rancor against Bush, could barely be distinguished from the realist and/or liberal internationalist positions of Brzezinski, Scowcroft, and just about every other member of the old foreign policy establishment. Unlike the realists but like many of the liberal internationalists, Fukuyama still believed in the ends of the Bush Doctrine, but the means he proposed to those ends—increased reliance on diplomacy and greater deference to the UN—were no different from the ones supported by both schools of thought. Nor did he make any more persuasive a case than they ever could or did for thinking that such an approach would produce anything other than appeasement of an unappeasable enemy.

But if Fukuyama's ideological trajectory could have been predicted, what did come as a real surprise was the disillusionment with Bush that overtook a growing number of other neoconservatives as the fifth anniversary of 9/11 was drawing near. So deep did this go that a British journalist, writing in the summer of 2006, could say that, to them, "the words 'Rice' and 'Bush' have all but become the Beltway equivalent of barnyard expletives." But this rage against Bush was powered by the polar opposite of Fukuyama's. For him, the problem with the Bush Doctrine "lies not in its ends, which are as American as apple pie, but rather in the overmilitarized means by which it has sought to accomplish them."* By contrast, for the neoconservatives who made their disillusionment known some months later, the problem with the

---

* Interestingly, this was the same complaint that George F. Kennan made in the 1950s about the Truman administration's application of the containment strategy he himself had been the first to advocate. But just as Kennan's extraordinary effort to deny saying what he had said could easily be refuted by his own words, so could Fukuyama's revisionist interpretation of the neoconservative position.

Bush Doctrine was not the Bush Doctrine: it was Bush. In their despairing view, the Bush Doctrine was in the process of being killed off—not by the obdurate realities of the Middle East, and not by any conceptual flaws, and not by its enemies at home and abroad, but rather by its author's loss of nerve in seeing it through. As against Fukuyama, what they wanted was for Bush to be more, not less, aggressive, and they wanted it *now*.

Thus, in a passage that provoked George Will into declaring that neoconservatism was "a spectacularly misnamed radicalism," William Kristol, the editor of the *Weekly Standard*, advocated an immediate

> military strike against Iranian nuclear facilities. Why wait? Does anyone think a nuclear Iran can be contained? That the current regime will negotiate in good faith? It would be easier to act sooner rather than later. Yes, there would be repercussions—and they would be healthy ones, showing a strong America that has rejected further appeasement.

As it happened, not all neoconservatives favored military action against Iran, placing their bets instead on an internal insurrection that would topple the mullocracy and replace it with a democratic regime. But they too blamed Bush, not so much for appeasing Iran as for failing to do everything in his power to help the democratic opposition there. And they too were in a big hurry: "Faster please" were the words with which Michael Ledeen, perhaps the leading member of this group, ended every one of his many pieces on Iran.

To show that this alleged failure constituted a blatant betrayal of the Bush Doctrine, it was only necessary to quote the president's own words, such as these from his Second Inaugural:

> Today, America speaks anew to the peoples of the world. All who live in tyranny and hopelessness can know the United States will not ignore your oppression or excuse your oppressors. When you stand for your liberty, we will stand with you.

Democratic reformers facing repression, prison or exile can know: America sees you for who you are: the future leaders of your free country.

Much the same point as Ledeen's about Iran was made by Richard Perle, a prominent neoconservative with considerable experience in government. (He had been an assistant secretary of defense under Reagan and the chairman of the Defense Policy Board under George W. Bush.) "Why Did Bush Blink on Iran?," Perle asked in a piece in the *Washington Post*. His bitter answer was that the president, after insisting that we would not negotiate directly with Iran, had yielded to the State Department's wish "to join talks with Iran on its nuclear program," and in choosing to beat this "ignominious retreat," Bush had crushed the hopes his "soaring speeches" had once aroused in the young democratic dissidents of Iran.

Other neoconservatives focused on what they saw as other betrayals by Bush of his own doctrine. In his column in the *Los Angeles Times*, Max Boot singled out Egypt as a prime example of "the downsizing of President Bush's democracy-promoting agenda." Joshua Muravchik of the American Enterprise Institute, in a piece in the *Washington Post* entitled "A Democracy Policy in Ashes," likewise concentrated on "the bitter disappointment that Egypt's democrats feel over the apparent waning of the Bush administration's ardor for their course." Moving beyond Iran and Egypt, Michael Rubin, the editor of the *Middle East Quarterly*, began a piece in the *Philadelphia Inquirer* under the headline "Fight for Mideast Democracy Failing" by offering examples of how, thanks to the Bush Doctrine, "democracy took root in what many once dismissed as infertile ground," but ended by showing how, "in the face of Bush's reversal," democratic dissenters throughout the region, who had been emboldened by the president's pledge "to seek and support the growth of democratic movements," were now being silenced and repressed once again, while "U.S. allies who once considered reform now abandon it."

According to still other unhappy neoconservatives, it was not only in the Middle East that the administration, instead of working to carry out Bush's promise to "end tyranny in our world," had inexplicably pulled down this pillar of the Bush Doctrine by adopting a new policy of "coddling despots" like the repressive leaders of both Russia and China. North Korea made for a comparably strong argument that the third pillar—the pledge to move preemptively against gathering threats—had also been blasted out from under the Bush Doctrine. In an especially unkind cut, Nicholas Eberstadt, a neoconservative expert on that country, charged that Bush's policy toward the regime of Kim Jong Il was, if anything, worse than Clinton's:

> Apparently unwilling to move against North Korea's nuclear challenges by itself, and evidently incapable of fashioning a practical response involving allies and others, the Bush administration's response to Pyongyang's atomic provocations is today principally characterized by renewed calls for additional rounds of toothless diplomacy.

Kenneth Adelman, yet another strong partisan of the Bush Doctrine, added insult to injury by telling an interviewer that its day was done and that the administration's handling of North Korea (and Iran) amounted to "the triumph of Kerryism."

Finally, and for good measure, around the same time as the president was being attacked for undermining the first three pillars of the Bush Doctrine, and in the midst of the war that broke out in the summer of 2006 between Hezbollah and Israel, yet another neoconservative, Frank Gaffney of the Center for Security Policy, came along to accuse Bush of undermining the fourth pillar of his own doctrine. Never mind that Bush, in his response to that war, was still steering clear of the old moral equivalence between Israel and the forces trying to destroy it. Never mind that he was still emphasizing that Israel's struggle against Hezbollah was yet another front in the "broader struggle between freedom and terror that [was] unfolding across the region." Never mind that by openly identifying Hezbollah as a creature of Iran and Syria he was still placing Israel's conflict with the Palestinians in the larger context of the war that the Arab-Muslim world had been waging since 1947 to wipe the Jewish state off the map. Ignoring all this, Gaffney rested his case entirely on the diplomatic maneuvering of the Bush administration, which everyone else in the world recognized as an effort to buy the Israelis more time before a cease-fire was imposed, but which Gaffney interpreted as pressure on the Israelis to "negotiate with and try to appease [Islamofascist totalitarians] when they are in the Islamofascists' cross hairs."

My own heart—needless to say—was with those neoconservatives who were pressing for a more aggressive implementation of the Bush Doctrine. I even thought that there was at least some merit in many, or perhaps even most, of the arguments they offered to explain why they had decided that American foreign policy was no longer true to the doctrine's promises. Without denying that the president was still talking the talk, they contended that his actions demonstrated that he had ceased walking the walk; it was by stacking those actions up against his own language that they sought to justify the charge of, at best, a loss of nerve and, at worst, an outright betrayal of the goals they formerly believed he meant to pursue and to which they themselves remained as dedicated as ever.

Nevertheless, I thought they were wrong—less wrong than the old foreign policy establishment, which agreed with them that the president had abandoned his own doctrine and which was gleeful instead of angry about it, but still wrong.

To begin with, the neoconservatives who had given up on Bush or were in the process of doing so overlooked one simple consideration: that he was a politician. This ridiculously obvious truth was obscured by the fact that Bush so often sounded like an ideologue—or perhaps *idealist* would be a better word. But here an old Jewish joke applied that I used to tell in connection with the same mistake that was also made about Ronald Reagan.

"Why are you dressed like that?" asks the Jewish mother of her son when he visits her wearing the uniform of a naval officer. "Because, Mama," he explains, "I just bought a boat, and I'm the captain." To which, smiling fondly, she replies, "Well, by you, you're a captain. And by me, you're a captain. But by a captain, are you a captain?" Which was to say that, like Ronald Reagan before him, George W. Bush might be an ideologue "by" most politicians, but "by" an ideologue he was no ideologue.

In other words, while he was certainly driven by ideas and ideals to a far greater extent than were most politicians, in implementing these ideas and ideals he was still subject to the same pressures by which all other politicians were constrained: pressures coming at him that, as president, he could ignore only at the peril of totally alienating the support his policies needed both at home and abroad if they were to be sustained. And what this, in turn, meant was that prudential considerations inevitably came into play whenever a major decision had to be made.

There were utopians to whom pursuing a principled or idealistic policy necessarily precluded the prudential judgment that determined which fights to pick at a given moment and which to delay until the time was ripe, when to pause and when to advance, and which tactic was the right one to use in maneuvering on a particular front. There were also realists who took the necessity of prudential judgment as proof that a policy driven by ideals was altogether incapable of being executed and could only lead to disaster if its proponents were naive enough to try putting it into practice.

None of this meant that those of us who shared Bush's ideas and ideals, but who labored under neither utopian nor realist delusions, were barred from questioning the soundness of his prudential judgment in this or that instance. But by the same token, we had an intellectual responsibility to recognize and acknowledge that he had already taken those ideas and ideals much further than might have been thought possible, especially given the ferocity of the opposition they had encountered from all sides and the difficulties they had also met with in the field. Indeed, it was a measure of his enormous political skills that—at a time in 2004 when things were not looking all that good for the Bush Doctrine's prospects in Iraq—he had succeeded in mobilizing enough support for its wildly controversial principles to run on them for a second term and win.

Since then, just as might have been (and was) predicted, the Islamofascists had been fighting back even harder than before, and the successes they scored had understandably distressed Max Boot, Joshua Muravchik, Michael Ledeen, Michael Rubin, Richard Perle, and other like-minded neoconservatives (not to mention democratic activists in the Middle East like Saad Eddin Ibrahim). Beyond being distressed, they were also angry at George W. Bush for doing things (like relying on futile negotiations with Iran) that they believed helped trigger these setbacks and for failing to do the things (like putting more pressure for reform on Egypt) that could reverse them.

Yet it was by no means self-evident that the course urged upon Bush by his neoconservative critics in this or that instance was— all factors considered—necessarily right or viable. Paul Mirengoff of the blog Power Line, taking account of the role of prudential judgment in a variety of countries with differing circumstances, did a good job of defending Bush's record in this area against his neoconservative critics:

> In each instance, the administration tilts toward democracy, with the degree of the tilt dictated by its perception of our ability to control events and the viability of the status quo. . . . In short, the administration's policy in the Middle East is to attempt to promote democracy to just the extent that doing so makes sense in light of facts on the ground. Since these facts vary from situation to situation, so too do the manifestations of our policy.*

---

* Mirengoff would later develop doubts about his own analysis, but I would continue to find it persuasive.

Besides, as a glance at the website of the Middle East Media Research Institute (MEMRI) revealed, the reformist impulse aroused by the Bush Doctrine was still very much alive throughout the region. Which told us that not all those committed to reform had lost heart, as, according to Muravchik and Boot, some had done in Egypt (and not even everyone there, as recent demonstrations attested).

But even if it could have been shown that the disillusioned neoconservatives' judgment of "the facts on the ground" had been right in every instance, the really tremendous fact—the overriding fact—would remain that it was entirely thanks to the Bush Doctrine that the Middle East had been "unfrozen." And even if Bush himself were for one reason or another unable to advance the process of political change that his policies had set into motion, there would be no return to the old arrangements and the old ways—no return, to repeat the words of Fouad Ajami, "to the old pact with tyranny."

And what of the charge that the president had refused to extend the Bush Doctrine to Russia and China, in spite of its pledge to "end tyranny everywhere in our world"? The answer was that everyone knew, or should have known—just as everyone knew about the targets of analogous promises made by Franklin D. Roosevelt in World War II and John F. Kennedy in World War III—that the primary and immediate focus of the Bush Doctrine was on the tyrannies in the Middle East, not on every despotic regime on the face of the earth. And just as everyone understood during World War II that defeating the evil regime in Germany justified an alliance with the equally evil regime in the Soviet Union, so it should have been clear that our de facto alliance with Pakistan, a hotbed of Islamist radicalism, was necessary to the successful prosecution of the war against Islamofascism throughout the Middle East.

And Iran? Andrew McCarthy of the Foundation for the Defense of Democracies went so far as to blame Tehran's decision to unleash its proxy Hezbollah against Israel on the

American abandonment of the Bush Doctrine in favor of offering the kitchen sink to the mullahs in a surely futile plea that they drop their nuclear ambitions.

McCarthy described this alleged abandonment as "Bush Doctrine Out, Democracy Project In." But the "democracy project" was not a substitute for the Bush Doctrine. To repeat: it was one of its animating or foundational principles. McCarthy was free to think that the fight against terrorism ought to have been given priority over democratization, and he might even have been right. But he was wrong in ascribing this view to the Bush Doctrine.

Still, there was no denying that Bush's dealings with Iran seemed to belie one of his most forceful early statements about such negotiations—one of those I quoted above in a different context:

> We cannot defend America and our friends by hoping for the best. We cannot put our faith in the word of tyrants, who solemnly sign nonproliferation treaties, and then systematically break them.

But it beggared belief that Bush had decided to go along with the European approach to Iran because he had suddenly discovered that there was wisdom in "hoping for the best" and putting "our faith in the word of tyrants." *Pace* Richard Perle, it seemed more likely that he was once again walking the last diplomatic mile, exactly as when he spent so many months and so much energy working to get the UN to endorse an invasion of Iraq. If so, the purpose, now as then, would be to expose the futility of diplomacy where the likes of Saddam Hussein and the Iranian mullocracy were concerned and to show that the only alternative to accepting the threats they posed was military action.

Robert Kagan—a neoconservative who had not given up on Bush—put this well in describing the negotiations as "giving futility its chance." Kagan also entertained the possibility that the negotiations were not merely a ploy on Bush's part and that his "ideal outcome really would be a diplomatic solution in which Iran voluntarily and verifiably abandoned its [nuclear] program." However that might be, once having played out the diplomatic string, Bush would be in a strong political position to say, along with Senator John McCain, that the only thing worse than bombing Iran would be allowing Iran to build a nuclear bomb—and not just to endorse that assessment but to act on it.

The problem of North Korea was different. In 1994, before the Clinton administration (working through—who else?—Jimmy Carter) accepted the so-called Agreed Framework, North Korea could have been stopped by military means from going nuclear. But precisely because the Agreed Framework had predictably failed, military action—difficult though still possible in the case of Iran—was no longer an option against a North Korea now armed with nuclear weapons. The only remaining hope was that its neighbors, and especially China and Japan, would in their own interests force it to disarm by threatening to cut off the aid through which the Kim Jong Il regime remained afloat. This was clearly what Bush was trying to accomplish, and, thin as the prospect of success might have been, it was hard to see what else he could have done short of risking a resort by North Korea to its nuclear weapons.

CHAPTER THIRTEEN

BUSH, REAGAN, AND TRUMAN

IN THINKING ABOUT George W. Bush's neoconservative critics, I was guided by the lesson I had learned from the fate of my own very similar criticisms of Ronald Reagan: not the hagiographical Reagan celebrated in conservative song and story, but the real Reagan, the Reagan who both did and failed to do many things that his idolatrous admirers had chosen to forget.

The first critique I produced was published early in Reagan's first term. This was a long article for the *New York Times Magazine* to which its editors gave the ungainly title "The Neoconservative Anguish over Reagan's Foreign Policy." Then, just as his second term was beginning, I wrote another long article, this one for *Foreign Affairs*, called "The Reagan Road to Détente." I also kept up a steady barrage of criticism in a syndicated column I was doing in those days.

It was as a passionate advocate of Reagan's declaratory policies that I repeatedly blasted him for one betrayal after another: for reacting tepidly to the suppression (yes, by the evil empire) of the anti-Communist Solidarity movement in Poland; for permitting his ambassadors behind the Iron Curtain to distance themselves from the genuinely democratic dissidents in those countries while cultivating the "reformist" proponents of "Communism with a human face"* (yes, much the same complaint that was now being made against Bush by democratic dissidents in Egypt and elsewhere); for cutting and running when Hezbollah (yes, the same Hezbollah with which Israel was now at war) blew up a barracks in Lebanon, killing 241 American servicemen; for trading arms for hostages with Iran (yes, the same mullocratic Iran we were confronting today); for entering into arms control negotiations with the Soviet Union (yes, the same species of negotiation at which he had once scoffed as a dangerous delusion spawned by détente).

Rereading those pieces, I was amazed to discover that they were right in almost every detail even though they were dead wrong about the ultimate effect. For what these acts of Reagan's turned out to be was a series of prudential tactics within an overall strategy that in the end succeeded in attaining its great objective.

At the certain risk of offending worshipers of the hagiographical Reagan, some of whom were in the habit of using him as a stick with which to beat up on Bush, I now confessed in print that the betrayals of which the latter was being accused seemed to me much less serious than those committed by his historical predecessor. But less serious or not, these supposed betrayals, too, deserved to be regarded as prudential tactics within an overall strategy.

And there was another consideration that needed to be taken into account. By the time Reagan became president, we had been fighting World War III for thirty-three years; by contrast, we started to fight World War IV only after Bush entered the White House. In this respect, it was not Reagan to whom Bush should have been compared, but Harry Truman.

To recapitulate: in 1947, at a time when many denied that the Soviet Union was even a threat to us, Truman saw it as an aggressive totalitarian force that was plunging us into another world war. If Truman had done nothing else than this, he would deserve

---

* I first learned about this from the great Soviet dissident Vladimir Bukovsky, whose report was bitterly confirmed by Vaclav Havel and other members of the Charter '77 group with whom I subsequently met in Prague.

to be ranked as a great president. But he did more: he also recognized that this new world war differed from the two that had preceded it and that it could not be fought in the same ways, or in as brief a time. Out of these two recognitions flowed the Truman Doctrine, and out of that doctrine came the new strategy known as containment.

The similarities with Bush were very striking. Even after 9/11, many pooh-poohed the threat of Islamofascism and, seeing its terrorist weaponry as merely a police matter, denied (and would continue to deny) that we were even really at war, much less in a new world war. But Bush understood that Islamofascism was "the heir of all the murderous ideologies of the twentieth century"—an aggressive totalitarian force that, like Nazism and communism before it, could be defeated only through a worldwide struggle. It was a struggle that, in its duration and in its mix of military and nonmilitary means, would be more like World War III than World War II. But it would also carry novel features with which containment had not been designed to cope. To quote Bush himself on this crucial point yet again:

> Containment is not possible when unbalanced dictators with weapons of mass destruction can deliver those weapons or missiles or secretly provide them to terrorist allies.

Out of these twin understandings, Bush promulgated his own doctrine, and out of that doctrine came the new military strategy of preemption and the new political strategy of democratization.

At a point in World War III comparable in certain respects to the one we had reached by the end of year five of World War IV, Harry Truman said this: "What a nation can and must do begins with the willingness and ability of its people to shoulder the burden." It turned out, despite innumerable indications to the contrary, that the American people of that era were indeed willing and able to shoulder the burden. But was it true about the American people of this era?

A hopeful answer to that question could be inferred from the election of 2004, when 62 million Americans voted to give George W. Bush another four years as their president. During the campaign, in the midst of an assault on the Bush Doctrine and on its author's character and competence that reached record levels of vituperation, and in spite of setbacks in Iraq that posed a serious threat to his reelection, Bush never yielded an inch. Instead of scurrying for protective cover from the assault, he stood out in the open and countered by reaffirming his belief in the soundness of the doctrine as well as his firm intention to stick with it in the years ahead. Over and over again he promised that he would stay the course in Iraq; that he would go on working for the spread of liberty throughout the greater Middle East (and democratic reform plus the renunciation of terrorism as the conditions for the establishment of a Palestinian state); that he would continue reserving the right to take preemptive military action against what in his best judgment were gathering dangers to the security of this country; and that to defend against those dangers he would never subject himself to "a global test" (as Kerry called it) by seeking permission from any other nation or nations before taking military action.

Surely those who voted for Bush in 2004 had every reason to know that he meant to go on fighting the war in the same way and under the guidance of the same principles. Nevertheless, no sooner had the ballots been counted than his liberal opponents began denying that the election amounted to a ratification of the Bush Doctrine. To the extent that they had any evidence for this claim, it derived from the widely publicized National Election Pool (NEP) exit poll. According to this poll, more voters (22 percent of the sample) had been motivated by a concern with moral values than by anything else, and it was among these voters that Bush had done best against Kerry; while he had also won overwhelmingly among the smaller group (19 percent) who were mainly worried about terrorism, he had lost by a correspondingly large margin with the still smaller proportion (15 percent) who chose

Iraq as their paramount concern. Armed with these numbers, the liberals had been only too happy to join (possibly for the first and last time) with the spokesmen for various groups on the religious Right in claiming that Bush had won because of the "faith factor" and the mobilization of the faithful around "family issues, including marriage [and] life."

Yet it was not at all obvious that the vague category of "moral values" had been taken by the people who participated in the NEP survey merely as embracing abortion and gay marriage alone. On the contrary: in all probability they understood it more broadly to mean the traditionalist culture in general.

Support for this interpretation came from James Webb (secretary of the Navy in the Reagan administration and a future Democratic candidate for the Senate who would run on a strongly anti-Bush platform). Webb had been arguing, convincingly, that this traditionalist culture was rooted in and still fed by the Scots-Irish ethnic group that constituted a very large proportion of the population of the "red" states that had gone for Bush. It was a group, he wrote, whose members were "family-oriented"; they "measure[d] leaders by their personal strength and values"; they had "a two-thousand-year-old military tradition"; and they were "deeply patriotic, having consistently supported every war America ha[d] fought, and [were] intensely opposed to gun control."

Looked at in this light, what the NEP poll revealed was that the "moral values" voters had in effect been endorsing the very qualities needed in a wartime leader. It was therefore reasonable to conclude that these voters should be added to, and not posed against, the large percentage that had supported Bush on the issue of terrorism. And there was equal justification for inferring that antiwar zealots must have been heavily represented among the 15 percent for whom Iraq was the burning issue, and that this (along with the influence of the negative media coverage) explained why Bush had lost out by a great margin to John Kerry with that group of voters.

The upshot was that on November 2, 2004, a clear majority of the American people were expressing their confidence in George W. Bush as the right man to lead us in a new time of war and in the policies he had enunciated through the Bush Doctrine and already put into practice as the right way to fight that war.

This, however, was very far from the whole story. For if 62 million Americans had said yes to Bush on November 2, another 59 million had shouted no. Nor were these 59 million—or at any rate their leaders in the Democratic Party and the wider liberal community—ready to admit defeat. After a brief period of sulking, the coalition of forces arrayed against Bush picked itself up off the ground and went after him with the desperate ferocity of a wounded tiger.

At the same time, there was a slow leakage of energy among Bush's supporters. Because of the growing disillusionment with Bush among conservative intellectuals, the balance of power in the world of ideas kept shifting in favor of the liberals. And the same disillusionment was having a trickle-down effect of its own on public opinion and derivatively on the Republicans in the House and Senate.

As the majority party in both bodies, the Republicans were still able to keep the Democrats at bay on the war. But many Republicans were disgruntled with Bush's domestic policies on issues like government spending and immigration, and this tended to spill over into their feelings about his conduct of the war. Worse yet, their own constituents back home were disheartened by the media spin on Iraq, and they were also misled by the treatment of Iraq as an isolated and self-contained war rather than as a front or a theater or a battle in the wider war against Islamofascism. The president and his people tried to correct these twin misimpressions and often did so in eloquent speeches, but with fewer and fewer reinforcements from the world of ideas, they were having more and more trouble in making themselves heard through an increasingly raucous antiwar din. The net result was that approval of Bush's handling of the war kept dropping in the public opinion polls, which in turn weakened the resolve of his own party to back him in staying the course.

Nothing, however—neither the polls nor the antiwar forces nor the conservative defeatists—could or would weaken George W. Bush's own resolve to stay the course—not only on the Iraqi front but in World War IV as a whole. But could he, in the two years he had left as president, carry the American people with him?

EPILOGUE

A S I TOLD you in the prologue, dear reader, I began this book in the months leading up to the fifth anniversary of World War IV. Now, as I start on the epilogue, September 11, 2006, is almost here and will have arrived, give or take a week or two, just when I reach the end of this account of the first five years of our entry into World War IV. But by the time you read these words, the sixth anniversary of 9/11 will either be hard upon you or will already have come and gone, and many things will have happened that neither I nor anyone else can possibly foresee. Depending on how they develop and turn out, it is conceivable that a definitive answer will by then have been given to the largest and most consequential of all the questions that have been raised in the past five years—the question of whether the Americans of this generation will turn out to be as willing and as able to bear the burden of World War IV as their forebears were in World War II and then again in World War III. But my guess is that this question will still be hanging in an unanswered state a year or more from now. I also think that even if it should come to seem settled one way or the other, it will repeatedly be reopened in response to the changing fortunes of war. Certainly this was how it went in World War III.

True, the burden of fighting World War IV differs from the one

Americans were asked to shoulder in World War III. But so did the burden of World War III differ from that of World War II. In some ways we today have it easier than the Americans who lived through those two wars. Rightly or wrongly, and for better or worse, this time there is no draft, there are no shortages or rationing, and taxes have not been raised. But on the other hand, we have more cause to be anxious over the safety and security of our continental homeland, which none of our enemies in those earlier wars ever managed to strike, let alone with the weapons of mass destruction that the Islamofascist terrorists may well get their hands on before this war is over.

Furthermore, because it will almost certainly go on for three or four decades, Americans of this generation are called upon to be far more patient than "the greatest generation" needed to be in World War II, in which the United States was involved for only four years. And facing an enemy in the Islamofascists who is even more elusive than the Communists, the American people of today are required to summon at least as much perseverance as the American people of those days did—for all their bitching and moaning—over the forty-two long years of World War III. Indeed, in this area the generation of World War IV has an even more difficult row to hoe than its predecessors in World War II and World War III.

The same is true in the area of morale. I have already noted that in the run-up to our entry into World War II there was a good deal of antiwar sentiment coming from isolationists and pacifists, but that hardly any of it survived Pearl Harbor. Nor, once we were in the war, was there any visible or openly expressed defeatism, not even in response to actual defeats—and we suffered many, especially in the early years. Nor was there a fixation on the mistakes made by Roosevelt and Churchill—and great men though they indubitably were, it bears repeating that they made many. It also bears repeating that some of their mistakes were so large and consequential that by comparison those of which the Bush administration stands accused seem insignificant, even if we stipulate for the sake of argument that the critics of today are right on every single point. Just think—to elaborate on only one example—of the incredible intelligence and command blunders leading up to the Battle of the Bulge that in only forty-four days cost more than nineteen thousand American lives (not to mention more than forty-seven thousand wounded, another twenty-three thousand captured or missing, and an untold number left with gangrenous feet because they had not been properly equipped for the brutal winter weather). Yet the main thing everyone knew and remembered about that terrible episode was that the American commander had responded to a German demand for surrender with the word "nuts."

In World War III, by contrast, great bouts of defeatist sentiment did get aroused by critics both of the Left (who thought we were being too aggressive) and of the Right (who thought we were not aggressive enough). Defeatism was also reinforced by angry recriminations over whether and/or how this or that battle should have been fought. And the battles in dispute were not only military, as in Korea and (to a much larger extent) Vietnam, but also political, as in the passionate debates over arms control and détente; in addition, they were ideological, as over the question of whether the enemy was Soviet expansionism in particular or communism in general, or our own paranoid delusions.

The first five years of World War IV have been marked by a version of all these features, but today the forces promoting defeatism are more powerful than they ever were in the past. Thinking of Iraq in particular, but not of Iraq alone, Amir Taheri describes the arsenal they command in terms that are all too accurate:

> The United States today has become home to a veritable industry of defeat—producing books, TV documentaries, research papers, intelligence analyses and feature movies destined for a growing market. Almost every day, some article appears assuming that the United States has already been defeated in Iraq, and recommending measures to deal with the consequences of defeat. And when

the United States does something, it does it Big: The defeat industry is assuming a bewildering scale.

Furthermore, in nonstop television news and on the Internet, which magnify everything that goes wrong, or only appears to have gone wrong, the defeatists of today possess a very powerful amplifier that broadcasts their message far more widely and loudly than their predecessors in World War III could even have imagined doing.

In trying to convey a sense of the importance of this change, James Q. Wilson invites us to consider "how things would have looked if the current media posture about American military and security activities had been in effect during World War II." It is easy, he says, to imagine that happening:

> In the 1930s, after all, the well-connected America First Committee had been arguing for years about the need for America to stay out of "Europe's wars." Aware of these popular views, the House extended the draft by only a one-vote margin in 1941. Women dressed in black crowded the entrance to the Senate, arguing against extending the draft. Several hundred students at Harvard and Yale, including future Yale leader Kingman Brewster and future American president Gerald Ford, signed statements saying that they would never go to war. Everything was in place for a media attack on the Second World War.

Thankfully, as we know, no such attack ever took place, but here, Wilson continues, is how it might have sounded if today's customs had been in effect:

> December 1941. Though the press supports America's going to war against Japan after Pearl Harbor, several editorials want to know why we didn't prevent the attack by selling Japan more oil. Others criticize us for going to war with two nations that had never attacked us, Germany and Italy.

October 1942. The *New York Times* runs an exclusive story about the British effort to decipher German messages at a hidden site at Bletchley Park in England. One op-ed writer criticizes this move, quoting Henry Stimson's statement that gentlemen do not read one another's mail. Because the Bletchley Park code-cracking helped us find German submarines before they attacked, successful U-boat attacks increased once the Germans, knowing of the program, changed their code.

January 1943. After President Roosevelt and Prime Minister Churchill call for the unconditional surrender of the Axis powers, several newspapers criticize them for having closed the door to a negotiated settlement. The press quotes several senators complaining that the unconditional surrender policy would harm the peace process.

May 1943. A big-city newspaper reveals the existence of the Manhattan Project and its effort to build atomic weapons. In these stories, several distinguished scientists lament the creation of such a terrible weapon. After General Leslie Groves testifies before a congressional committee, the press lambastes him for wasting money, ignoring scientific opinion, and imperiling the environment by building plants at Hanford and Oak Ridge.

December 1944. The German counterattack against the Allies in the Ardennes yields heavy American losses in the Battle of the Bulge. The press gives splashy coverage to the Democratic National Committee chairman's assertion that the war cannot be won. A member of the House, a former Marine, urges that our troops be sent to Okinawa.

August 1945. After President Truman authorizes dropping the atomic bomb on Japan, many newspapers urge his impeachment.

We who believe in the absolute necessity of fighting and winning World War IV can complain all we like about the conditions that have bred so much defeatism, and from which our morale will continue to suffer to an extent undreamed of in World War II, and even more than it did in World War III. But these are the conditions under which World War IV will have to be fought if it is to be fought at all. And if it is to be fought at all, it will also have to be fought by the kind of people Americans now are. Before the United States entered World War II, serious doubts were raised as to whether we were a match for such disciplined and fanatical enemies as Nazi Germany and Imperial Japan. And in World War III, leading anti-Communists like Whittaker Chambers and James Burnham were sure that we lacked the stomach, the heart, the will, and the wit to stand effectively against the true believers of the Soviet Union and its allies and sympathizers: to Chambers we were "the losing side," and to Burnham we were veritably suicidal in our liberal weakness and folly. They turned out to be wrong because—as, just after the fall of the Berlin Wall, Charles Horner of the Hudson Institute would put it in speaking of Chambers—they, and not they alone, failed "to anticipate the resiliency of the American citizenry and its leadership." Today, as I write, similar doubts and fears are once again flying all over the place, with even some who would like to believe otherwise murmuring that we have all grown too soft, too self-indulgent, and too self-absorbed to meet an even more daunting challenge from an enemy who is so much readier to die for his beliefs than most of us are. It is also being said that we have grown so complacent since 9/11/2001 that nothing short of another terrorist attack here at home will shake us back into the realization that we are actually at war.

It would be foolish to deny that there is some basis for such doubts and fears. And yet it would surely be just as foolish to repeat the mistake of Chambers and Burnham in failing "to anticipate the resiliency of the American citizenry and its leadership." As to the citizenry, we need only point to the young Americans in uniform, all volunteers, who have been bearing the heaviest burden of World War IV. In their determination, their courage, and their love of country, they are by all accounts a match, and more than a match, for their forebears of World War II and World

War III. And who is to say that these young people are less representative of America than those of their elders and contemporaries who conspicuously lack the same virtues? Where did these young people come from, where were they bred and raised, and where did they absorb "the right stuff" if not the America of today? It is an America as invisible to the eyes of the liberal culture as it was in 1972 when Pauline Kael, the film critic of *The New Yorker*, notoriously wondered how Nixon could have won by a landslide when she knew not a single person who had voted for him. But this still invisible America still exists, even in some still invisible enclaves of New York City itself.

When, however, we turn to leadership—the other factor whose resiliency Horner said Chambers and Burnham underestimated—doubts like theirs are harder to avoid. Not, to say it again, that I for one have any doubts about the leadership of George W. Bush. In fact, I believe that on top of the ways in which he already resembles Harry Truman will come the belated recognition of him as a great president. Let me also reiterate my belief that this will happen even if he (yet again like Truman) should turn out to have been able to push his own doctrine just so far and no further. And in answer to the bitter complaints about his domestic policies— from the Right on government spending and immigration, and from the Left on such issues as Terry Schiavo and stem cell research—I ask, who today either remembers or cares about Truman's domestic policies? Finally, I believe that future historians will be mystified by the endlessly repeated complaint from conservatives today that Bush has failed to explain what this war is all about and what it will take to win it. For it will seem obvious in retrospect that he has done precisely that in a series of speeches among which are some of the greatest ever made by an American president (most notably the one to a joint session of Congress on September 20, 2001, and his even more luminous Second Inaugural Address).

So far as resiliency goes, a good measure of it is the buoyancy Bush has exhibited even during the darkest moments of his presidency and even when (another resemblance to Truman) his approval ratings were sinking to record lows. At this moment, with only about two years to go, he shows none of the usual symptoms of lame-duckery and all the signs of energy and resolve. But he *does* have only two years to go, and it is in speculating on who might succeed him that doubts begin to arise. Rudy Giuliani and John McCain are at this point the two Republican front-runners, and if either one of them should win in 2008, chances are that the Bush Doctrine will remain our guiding strategy. But suppose that a Democrat should become president in 2008. What then?

Here, once more, it will help to look back at Truman—this time to see how his doctrine fared while he was still in office, and what happened to it after he left.

When it was first enunciated in 1947, the Truman Doctrine was attacked from several different directions. On the Right, there were the isolationists who—after being sidelined by World War II—had made something of a comeback in the Republican Party under the leadership of Senator Robert Taft. Their complaint was that Truman had committed the United States to endless interventions that had no clear bearing on our national interest. But there was also another faction on the Right that denounced containment not as recklessly ambitious but as too timid. This group was still small, but within the next few years it would find powerful spokesmen in Republican political figures like Richard Nixon and John Foster Dulles and conservative intellectuals like William F. Buckley Jr. and James Burnham.

At the other end of the political spectrum were the Communists and their "liberal" fellow travelers who—strengthened by our alliance with the Soviet Union in World War II—had emerged as a relatively sizable group and would soon form a new political party behind Henry Wallace. In their view, the Soviets had more cause to defend themselves against us than we had to defend ourselves against them, and it was Truman, not Stalin, who posed the greater danger to "free peoples everywhere." But criticism also came from the political center, as represented by Walter

Lippmann, the most influential and most prestigious commentator of the period. Lippmann argued that Truman had sounded "the tocsin of an ideological crusade" that was nothing less than messianic in its scope.

In the election of 1948, Truman had the seemingly impossible task of confronting all three of these challenges (and a few others as well). When, against what every poll had predicted, he succeeded in warding them all off and in defeating the Republican candidate, Thomas E. Dewey, he could reasonably claim that the American people were behind the main principles of his foreign policy.

Even so, enough bitter opposition remained within and around the Republican Party to leave it uncertain as to whether containment was an *American* policy or only the policy of the Democrats. This uncertainty was exacerbated by the presidential election of 1952, when the Republicans behind Dwight D. Eisenhower ran against Truman's handpicked successor, Adlai Stevenson, in a campaign featuring strident attacks on the Truman Doctrine by Eisenhower's running mate, Richard Nixon, and his future secretary of state, John Foster Dulles. Nixon, for example, mocked Stevenson as a graduate of the "Cowardly College of Communist Containment" run by Truman's secretary of state, Dean Acheson, while Dulles repeatedly called for ditching containment in favor of a policy of "rollback" and "liberation." And both Nixon and Dulles strongly signaled their endorsement of General Douglas MacArthur's insistence that Truman was wrong to settle for holding the line in Korea instead of going all the way—or, as MacArthur had famously put it, "There is no substitute for victory."

Yet when Eisenhower came into office, he hardly touched a hair on the head of the Truman Doctrine. Far from adopting a bolder and more aggressive strategy, the new president ended the by then extremely unpopular Korean War on the basis of the status quo ante—in other words, precisely on the terms of containment. Even more telling was Eisenhower's refusal three years later to intervene when the Hungarians, apparently encouraged by the rhetoric of liberation still being employed in the broadcasts of Radio Free Europe, rose up in revolt against their Soviet masters. For better or worse, this finally dispelled any lingering doubt as to whether containment was the policy of just the Democratic Party. With full bipartisan support behind it, the Truman Doctrine had become the official policy of the United States of America.

The analogy is obviously not perfect, but the resemblances between the political battles that were fought in the first five years of World War III and the ones that have been fought in the first five years of World War IV are still very striking. If in January 2009 a Democrat should be sworn in as president of the United States, will he (or she—as for once reality in the shape of Hillary Clinton rather than political correctness demands that we add), like Eisenhower with respect to Republican derision of the Truman Doctrine in 1952, quietly shelve the frenetic attacks of the Democrats on the Bush Doctrine? Will he or she then tacitly acknowledge that there is no serious alternative to the strategy it prescribes other than returning to the law enforcement approach through which we dealt so ineffectually with terrorism before 9/11 and/or submitting to the craven will of the Europeans and the corrupt ministrations of the UN? Will he or she realize that no matter how such a shift might be dressed up and spun, it would—and rightly—be interpreted by our enemies as a cowardly retreat? Will he or she understand that the despotisms of the Middle East would then once again feel free to offer sanctuary and launching pads to Islamofascist terrorists? Will he or she realize that these terrorists would be emboldened to attack us again—and on an infinitely greater scale than before? And on the home front, will he or she cease and desist from raising false alarms about the threat to civil liberties posed by programs essential to protecting us from just such terrorist attacks—programs like the surveillance of certain international phone calls or the tracking of bank deposits? Will he or she stop defining "torture" down to the point where it becomes impossible to conduct any interrogation at all of captured terrorists, thereby depriving us of the intelligence that is also necessary if further attacks are to be prevented?

From the way the Democrats have been acting and speaking, especially since Bush's reelection in 2004, all of the answers would seem to be no. But is it too much to hope that these denials of reality are only the luxurious indulgences of opposition, and that a Democratic president will be forced by the awesome responsibilities of power to forgo them all and to take up where Bush will have left off?

Not that, if this were to happen, a perfect bipartisan harmony would descend upon the nation. After all, contrary to the roseate reminiscences of how it was then, not even the bipartisan consensus that was reached after 1952 eliminated all discord. Plenty of it remained, and it was periodically exacerbated by such reverses as Korea under Eisenhower and Iran under Carter, not to mention outright defeats like the Bay of Pigs under Kennedy and then Vietnam under Johnson, Nixon, and Ford. There was also a long stretch during which it looked as though our enemies were so strong, and we so debilitated, that many among us thought the best we could do was to in effect sue for a negotiated peace. Thus, in the late 1970s and early 1980s, an almost perfect storm of crises broke out, which, as John O'Sullivan of the *National Review* once summarized them,

> included two oil price hikes; massive worldwide stagflation; Soviet advances into Central America, Africa and Afghanistan; the Tehran hostage crisis; the loss of South Vietnam, leading to the "boat people" crisis; the spread of terrorism; the installation of Soviet missiles in Eastern Europe and the drift of the U.N. toward a Third World radicalism exemplified by its support for the so-called new world economic order of international socialist redistribution. Grievous though these crises were, almost the worst thing about them was the mood of despair they engendered. The idea that the West had embarked on an inevitable decline gripped elites. The Club of Rome forecast increasing shortages of raw materials that would lead to a drastic lowering of Western living standards.

All this was even worse and more humiliating (if not necessarily more consequential) than the worst-case scenario of a cut-and-run withdrawal from Iraq being urged upon us at this very moment by the political descendants of the antiwar activists and the defeatists of World War III. But (God be thanked) we eventually pulled ourselves up and out of the slough of despond, and because we did, we were rewarded with a victory that freed us from a military, political, and ideological threat. Moreover, to the people living both within the Soviet Union itself and in its East European empire, our victory brought liberation from a totalitarian tyranny. Admittedly, not everything came up roses immediately after liberation, but it would be ridiculous to contend that nothing changed for the better when communism landed on the very ash heap of history that Marx had predicted would be the final resting place of capitalism.

Suppose that we hang in long enough to carry World War IV to a comparably successful conclusion. What will victory bring this time around? To us it will bring the elimination of another, and in some respects greater, threat to our safety and security. And because that threat cannot be eliminated without "draining the swamps" in which it breeds, victory will also entail the liberation of another group of countries from another species of totalitarian tyranny. As we can already see from Afghanistan and Iraq, liberation will no more result in the overnight establishment of ideal conditions in the Middle East than it has done in East Europe or Russia. But as in East Europe, better things will immediately happen, and a genuine opportunity will be opened up for even better things to come.

Of course, many of Bush's critics question or totally reject the idea that democratization represents the best and perhaps even the only way to defeat Islamofascism and the terrorism it uses as its main weapon against us. Bush has placed his bet on a belief in the universality of the desire for freedom and for the prosperity that freedom produces. But what if he is wrong? What if the Middle East is incapable of democratization? What if the peoples of that region do not wish to be as free and as prosperous as we are? And what if Islam as a religion is by its very nature incompatible with democracy?

These are hard questions about which reasonable people can and do differ. But those of us who back Bush's bet have our own set of doubts about the doubts of the doubters. In addition to forgetting how recently the miserable despotisms of the Middle East were established, they seem to take it for granted that Arabs and/or Muslims are so different from most of their fellow human beings that they actually like being pushed around and repressed and beaten and killed by thugs, whether dressed in military uniforms or wearing clerical garb. For our part, we wonder whether Muslims really do prefer being poor and hungry and ill housed to enjoying the comforts and conveniences that we in the West take so totally for granted that we no longer remember to be grateful for them.

Fareed Zakaria of *Newsweek*, like many moderate critics of the Bush Doctrine, thinks that trying to establish democracy is premature:

> We do not seek democracy in the Middle East—at least not yet. We seek first what might be called the preconditions for democracy . . . —the rule of law, individual rights, private property, independent courts, the separation of church and state. . . . We should not assume that what took hundreds of years in the West can happen overnight in the Middle East.

Now, those of us who believe in the Bush Doctrine see nothing wrong with pursuing Zakaria's agenda. But neither do we agree that elections should necessarily wait upon the fulfillment of all these "preconditions." Yes, elections brought the terrorists of Hamas to power in the Palestinian Authority, gave the terrorists of Hezbollah a place in the Lebanese government, and awarded the terrorists of the Muslim Brotherhood seats in the Egyptian parliament. But we are impressed by what Amir Taheri, out of his deep knowledge of the region, has to say on this issue:

> Disappointed by the victory of Hamas in the Palestinian election and the strong showing of the Muslim Brotherhood in last year's

polls in Egypt, some doubt the wisdom of pushing for elections in the Muslim world. . . . The holding of elections, however, is a clear admission that the principal basis for legitimacy is the will of the people as freely expressed through ballot boxes. In well-established democracies, this may sound trite; in Arab societies, it is a revolutionary idea.

And we also take heart from Fouad Ajami's corroborative testimony that, "while the ballot is not infallible," it has "broken the pact with Arab tyranny."

In an excellent summation of our case, Victor Davis Hanson explains why the breaking of this pact with tyranny is as necessary and good for us as it is for the Middle East:

> We long tried almost everything else. Accepting dictators on their own terms did not bring stability, but constant war, oil embargoes, and terrorism from the 1960s onward. Replying to two decades of terrorist attacks, from the Iranian hostage taking in 1979 to the attack on the USS *Cole* in 2000, with indictments and a few cruise missiles only emboldened the jihadists. And staging coups or propping up authoritarians in Iran or the Gulf simply radicalized the Middle East.

Hanson then makes a surprising point about "what the U.S. is trying to do in the Middle East":

> In truth, fostering democracy in Afghanistan and Iraq was not our first, but our last choice. It was not a good option, only a bad one when the other alternatives had proven far worse.

Well, in my own opinion, bad as this option may have been by certain political standards, it was—and still is—marked by more than a touch of nobility. But I fully endorse Hanson's conclusion that "constitutional government" or "messy democracy" is the one course that might someday "free Middle Easterners from kidnappings, suicide bombers and dictators in sunglasses," while at the same time freeing us from the global reach of Islamic terrorism. In any event, according to Bernard Lewis, we have no choice: "Either," he says, "we bring them freedom, or they destroy us."

Those of us who support the Bush Doctrine believe that this case—the case (to revert one last time to my own preferred formulation of it) for making the Middle East safe for America by making it safe for democracy—is all but irrefutable. Extending it, we also take issue with the view that democracy—and capitalism—can grow only in a soil that has been cultivated for centuries. We often point out that in the aftermath of World War II, the United States managed within a single decade to transform both Nazi Germany and Imperial Japan into capitalist democracies. And in the aftermath of the defeat of communism in World War III, a similar process got under way on its own steam in Central and Eastern Europe, and even (before Vladimir Putin slammed on the brakes) in the old heartland of the evil empire itself. Furthermore, as we are reminded by Fouad Ajami (leaning here on the work of Samuel Huntington and Robert Dahl, two of the leading theorists of democracy in our time):

> In fifteen of the twenty-nine democratic countries in 1970, democratic regimes were midwifed by foreign rule, or had come into being right after independence from foreign occupation.

Why not the Muslim world? The realist answer is that things are different there. To which our answer is that things are different everywhere, and a thousand reasons to expect the failure of any enterprise can always be conjured up to discourage making an ambitious effort.

Listen again to Bernard Lewis, who says this about the common view that "Islamic peoples are incapable of decent civilized government": "It shows ignorance of the Arab past, contempt for the Arab present, and unconcern for the Arab future." Lewis's own view is that

> Arab ways are different from our ways. They must be allowed to develop in accordance with their cultural principles, but it is pos-

sible for them—as for anyone else, anywhere in the world, with discreet help from outside and most specifically from the United States—to develop democratic institutions of a kind.

To this, in turn, the counter frequently is "Look at Iraq." The Bush administration, misled by neocons like us, wildly underestimated the special difficulties of democratizing Iraq, even assuming it to be possible at all. Yet talk about a "cakewalk" and the like mainly came from outside the administration; in any event it was applied to the future military campaign (which definitely did turn out to be a cakewalk), not to the ensuing reconstruction of Iraq. As to the latter, I confess to having been among those who failed to anticipate the ferocity of the opposition to democratization that would develop and therefore how long so great a transformation would take. But like the president, I remained convinced that it could and would be achieved if we could "stay the course" for (in the words of Secretary of Defense Donald Rumsfeld) "as long as it takes and not a day longer." How long would that be? For those who opposed the Bush Doctrine, a year (or even a month?) after the end of major combat operations was already much too much, and as I write they are now more and more openly demanding an early or even an immediate withdrawal; for those of us who continue to support the Bush Doctrine, "as long as it takes" means until the day when the Iraqis are able to assume the lion's share of responsibility for ensuring the irreversibility of the progress they have already made toward the establishment of a loosely federated republic that still seems, given the stakes, the only satisfactory formula.

As with democratization, so with the reform and modernization of Islam. In considering this even more difficult question, we find ourselves asking whether Islam can really go on for all eternity resisting the kind of reformation and modernization that began within Christianity and Judaism in the early modern period. Not that we are so naive as to imagine that Islam can be reformed overnight, or from the outside. In its heyday, Islam was able to impose itself on large parts of the world by the sword; there is no chance today of an inverse instant transformation of Islam by the force of American arms.

There is, however, at least a fighting chance that a clearing of the ground and a sowing of the seeds out of which new political, economic, and social conditions can grow will gradually give rise to correlative religious pressures from within. Such pressures would take the form of an ultimately irresistible demand on theologians and clerics to find warrants in the Qur'an and the *shari'a* under which it would be possible to remain a good Muslim while enjoying the blessings of decent government, and even of political and economic liberty. In this way a course might finally be set toward the reform and modernization of the Islamic religion itself.

But what about us here in America? On what course are we now set?

In his first State of the Union address, President Bush tried to answer that question by affirming that *history* had called America to action and that it was both "our responsibility and our privilege to fight freedom's fight"—a fight he also characterized as "a unique opportunity for us to seize." A few years later, he reminded us that "we did not seek this war on terror," but that, having been sought out by it, we responded, and now we were trying to meet the "great demands" that "history has placed on our country."

In this language, and especially in the repeated references to history, we can hear an echo of the concluding paragraphs of George F. Kennan's "X" essay, written at the outbreak of World War III:

> The issue of Soviet-American relations is in essence a test of the overall worth of the United States as a nation among nations. To avoid destruction the United States need only measure up to its own best traditions and prove itself worthy of preservation as a great nation.

Kennan then went on to his peroration:

> In the light of these circumstances, the thoughtful observer of Russian-American relations will experience a certain gratitude for

a Providence which, by providing the American people with this implacable challenge, has made their entire security as a nation dependent on their pulling themselves together and accepting the responsibilities of moral and political leadership that history plainly intended them to bear.

Substitute "Islamofascism" for "Russian-American relations," and every other word of this magnificent statement applies to us as a nation today. In 1947 we accepted the responsibilities of moral and political leadership that history "plainly intended" us to bear, and for the next forty-two years we acted on them. We may not always have acted on them wisely or well, and we often did so only after much kicking and screaming. But act on them we did. We thereby ensured our own "preservation as a great nation," while also bringing a better life to millions upon millions of people in a major region of the world.

Now "our entire security as a nation"—including, to a greater extent than in 1947, our physical security—once more depends on whether we are willing to accept and ready to act upon the responsibilities of moral and political leadership that history has yet again so squarely placed upon our shoulders. Furthermore, and also to a greater extent than in 1947, it is almost entirely on *our* shoulders that the burden rests. Then we had (more or less) willing allies throughout the West, but this time it is (to borrow from the title of a book by Mark Steyn about the slow demographic suicide of Western Europe) "America alone" on which victory in World War IV depends. Conceivably the prospect of being conquered from within by Islamofascism will so concentrate the minds of the major West European countries that they will eventually join us in the fight against the threat from without. It is a consummation devoutly to be wished, but not, alas, one on which we can reasonably or prudently count.

And so the question comes back to us—to America alone. Is this country "ready to measure up to its own best traditions and prove itself worthy of preservation as a great nation"? Do we, the

American people of this generation, have it in us to beat back the "implacable challenge" of Islamofascism as the "greatest generation" of World War II did in taking on the Nazis and their fascist allies, and as its children and grandchildren ultimately managed to do in confronting the Soviet Union and its Communist empire in World War III? In spite of how bleak the prospects look, as of September 11, 2006, I persist in thinking that we do and that we will, but the jury is still out, and it will not return a final verdict for some time to come.

ACKNOWLEDGMENTS

IN WRITING THIS BOOK I drew freely on several of my own past works, most of them articles I did for *Commentary*, to whose editor, Neal Kozodoy, they—and I—owe a great debt. I owe a comparable debt to Adam Bellow of Doubleday, whose editorial suggestions were an invaluable help to me in the process out of which the book emerged—a process of integrating some sections of my earlier efforts into different settings; updating, adapting, and reworking others; and weaving them all together with entirely new material. Finally, I wish to thank my agents, Glen Hartley and Lynn Chu, whose initiative is what got me going in the first place.

INDEX